CONTRACEPTION

——— AND THE ———

ORTHODOX CHURCH

CONTRACEPTION

—— AND THE ——

ORTHODOX CHURCH

WITH THE 1937 AND 1978 ENCYCLICALS OF
THE CHURCH OF GREECE

Book layout and cover design by Andrew Ritchey,
The Orthodox Design Company
www.orthodoxdesigncompany.com

Contraception and the Orthodox Church
ISBN: 978-1-965379-01-1

Patristic Nectar
www.patristicnectar.org
info@patristicnectar.org

Contents

Foreword

In reading this carefully researched and argued short book on the topic of artificial contraception, I thought back happily to that time when its author was a student at the Holy Cross seminary. In both the lecture hall and in his written work, it was clear that Tikhon was already becoming a true scholar of the patristic tradition, as well as a patient and kind dialogue partner.

The research paper that became this book, in particular, resonated as something deeper and more grounded than we normally encounter on this important subject. I hoped then and am glad now that this work will receive a wider readership.

Other memories, melancholy ones, are called to mind by the topic itself, however. Long ago, when I was just a second grader, I had the chance to read a nonfiction children's story about the young indigenous man who had done so much to save the Pilgrims. I distinctly recall the late afternoon when, reading the book on my bed at home in the dying light, I arrived at the passage where young Squanto at last returned to the homeland of his own Wampanoag people.

After years of first captivity and then freedom in Spain and England, Squanto arrived back in Massachusetts to discover that his native people had been the victims of a plague so devastating that none of their number remained. His own people were gone—a foreshadowing of the tragic fate of most of the tribes once native to the regions east of the Mississippi.

The sadness that filled my young eyes with tears then has returned now in greater force. All across the world, we see nation after nation and people after people undergoing an alarming collapse of human fertility.

This global rejection of childbearing is an existential crisis threatening the very survival of humanity. Should current trends continue for a few decades more, which they seem likely to do, humanity will witness the onset of numerous local dark ages from which some people groups, languages, and civilizations are likely never to reemerge.

The discovery and uncritical adoption of mass produced artificial contraception is turning out to be part of a looming extinction level event for the human race—and one that until very recently has somehow gone unnoticed, unremarked, and certainly not engaged with in the seriousness which it deserves, by Christian theologians. Modernity is proving to be unsustainable, in the most basic demographic sense.

The time has passed when we could paper over the painful role played by the easy embrace of artificial contraception, and by the general failure of Christian theologians to speak in a mature and balanced way about its moral dimensions and spiritual impact, in this unfolding catastrophe. For some nations, in fact, it may already be too late.

How did this happen? How have things come to this?

In the immediate aftermath of the First World War, it seemed to some that the best chance for human survival lay in drastically limiting the number of human beings born into the world. To this end, in 1929 the Anglican Church, the religion of the greatest imperial power ever to have existed to that time, became the first Christian church in history to endorse the use of artificial contraception.

Looking back, we can see that the apologists for artificial contraception took it for granted that there would always be "enough" people. A little later, modern society more generally took it for granted that fornication and adultery could somehow be managed, even at the industrial scale in which we practiced them, without grave injury to Christian societies. Together, we turned our eyes from the abyss of abortion, experimented with the idea that the family was optional, and toyed with the devastating belief that the blessing of bodily gender was in fact a curse.

And behind all of this we failed to note the iconoclasm and gnosticism, not to mention the element of cruelty, encoded within the systems with which we moderns organize and even think about our social lives and our world.

Less than a century after the first Christian approval of artificial contraception, as much of the human race seems ready to consign itself slowly to oblivion, one broken heart and one fruitless union at a time, we must consider more carefully exactly what the Orthodox Christian tradition has bequeathed to us about the purpose of marriage and the calling to create life. What Dr. Pino has to say, and the skill with which he says it, are a good place to start.

It must also be stressed that when we experience the spiritual penthos of which I spoke earlier, we are not to join our own darkened intellects nor our own passionate emotions of despair to this divine gift of purifying sadness. Neither, though, are we to interrupt its germination through false hopes and shallow optimisms.

Rather, we are to understand the sacred gift of penthos for what it is—a green shoot, to be watered by tears of repentance, of the new life being planted in us by God. It is through exactly such spiritual sadness, oftentimes, that the heart continues to be born again in Christ by the Holy Spirit.

As grim as things now appear for human fertility and demography, we are yet commanded to believe and to hope that our grief for the not yet vanished nations and races of the world, and our cries for divine mercy upon them, will be heard by our good and loving God. And we hope that if not this generation, then perhaps the next, will have the divinely given strength to hear the moral voice of the Church Fathers clearly and soberly, and in all areas of life.

Timothy Patitsas, Ph.D.
Brookline, Mass.

Introduction

St Gregory of Nyssa, in his letter to Heracleianus, points out that the Christian life contains two elements: "the ethical part," whereby we are enjoined to keep the commandments and so remedy our lives, and "the precision of dogmas," whereby we maintain an Orthodox confession of faith.[1] Both elements, Gregory tells us, were transmitted by Christ through the apostles. Both elements are also essential for an Orthodox Christian life, because we *work out our salvation*, as St Paul describes it (Phil 2:12), not only by proclaiming a technically accurate theology, but also, and especially, by living as the Lord calls us to live.[2] For, *Not every one that says unto Me, 'Lord, Lord,' shall enter*

---

[1] St. Gregory of Nyssa, Epistle 24.2: τὸ ἠθικὸν μέρος καὶ τὴν τῶν δογμάτων ἀκρίβειαν (Gregorii Nyseni Opera 8.2: Epistulae, ed. Giorgio Pasquali [Leiden: Brill, 1959], 75). These two elements, the moral and the dogmatic, correspond to the two injunctions of the Great Commission (Mt 28:18–20), wherein the apostles are told to make disciples of all nations by (A) *baptizing them in the name of the Father and of the Son and of the Holy Spirit*, and (B) *teaching them to observe all that I commanded you.*

[2] This is not salvation through the works or doing of the Law (earned salvation), but rather a genuine Christian life in obedience to the Lord's commandments, *Who will render to each according to his deeds* (Rom 2:6). The idea that we will be held to account for the way we live is especially evident in the parable of the sheep and the goats in Matthew 25:31–46, which speaks

into the kingdom of heaven, but he that does the will of My Father which is in heaven (Mt 7:21).

Among the most recent and widespread moral challenges faced by Orthodox Christians has been the rapid growth, dissemination, and normalization of contraception across nearly all sectors of society in the last two centuries. Contraception, understood as the deliberate prevention of conception *during the marital act*, whether through mechanical, pharmaceutical, or other means, naturally touches on the most intimate parts of human life. It not only impacts the conjugal life of spouses and the character of family life, but also, in many cases, entails economic and medical questions, to say nothing of the ramifications for human population and demographics. All of these factors contribute to making contraception, at once, controversial, sensitive, and deeply consequential.

Although contraceptive devices and techniques are by no means new, contraception as we know it today, as a feature of modern medicine and public life, dates only to the late nineteenth century. After the opening of the first birth control clinic in Amsterdam in 1882 by Aletta Jacobs, and thanks to the activism of eugenicists like

---

of punishment and reward in accordance with one's actions in this life. It is also laid out explicitly in James 2:14–26.

Margaret Sanger and Marie Stopes, developed nations grappled for decades with the issue of contraception, often in bitter polemics and a protracted culture war. By the 1920s, a revolution in public morality had begun to take firm root,[3] and in 1930, at its seventh Lambeth Conference, the Anglican Church amended its resolutions from a decade earlier to give official ecclesiastical approbation, for the first time in human history, to the use of contraceptives.

Today, contraception is widely accepted, if not normative, in most secular societies, cultures, and communities of the world. This is true not only in the so-called West, but in nearly all cultures and civilizations around the globe, including, especially, places like Russia, Iran, and China.[4] Where contraception continues to be rejected, opponents most often cite religious principles or concerns, though they remain in a global minority.[5]

---

[3] For an overview, see Donna J. Drucker, *Contraception: A Concise History* (Cambridge, MA: MIT Press, 2020).

[4] The restrictions on childbirth in China are well known. On contraception in the Middle East, see Farrokh Habibzadeh, *The Lancet* 380 (2012): 1. On the rise of contraception in post-Soviet Russia, where it replaced abortion as the birth control method of choice, see Anatoly Vishnevsky et al., "The Contraceptive Revolution in Russia," *Демографическое обозрение* [*Demographic Review*] 4.5 (2017): 86–108.

[5] See Wade M. Cole and Claudia Geist, "Conceiving of Contraception: World Society, Cultural Resistance, and Contraceptive

In the context of a specifically Christian morality, the rejection of contraception today is widely associated almost exclusively with the Roman Catholic Church, which condemned the practice in two landmark encyclicals: *Casti Connubii*, issued in 1930 by Pius XI, and *Humanae Vitae*, issued in 1968 by Paul VI. The 'official' position of the Orthodox Church remains much less clear.

Yet if the proclamation of the Gospel and the living of a Christian life contain an ethical component in addition to "the precision of dogmas," it is surely not unreasonable for married couples, and for the clergy who guide them, to seek a moral resolution to the questions surrounding contraception in the tradition of the Church. Is contraception a morally acceptable part of marriage, or does it offend Orthodox Christian sensibilities? What do our Fathers tell us? Scholars over the last several decades, to say nothing of the ongoing debate and controversy at the popular level, have attempted to answer this question. Writers like Chrysostom Zaphiris, Philip Sherrard, John Meyendorff, Paul Evdokimov,

---

Use, 1970–2012," *Social Forces* 99.4 (2021): 1394–1431. On the hesitancy over the effects of hormonal contraception, in particular, for non-religious reasons, see Mireille Le Guen et al., "Reasons for Rejecting Hormonal Contraception in Western Countries: A Systematic Review," *Social Science and Medicine* 284 (2021): 114–247.

and others, are among the most prominent scholars to have offered their thoughts and analysis on what an authentic Orthodox Christian approach to contraception is or should be. Yet most of the existing studies on this question remain deficient. To begin, we still possess no comprehensive study of the question, with most treatments being limited to a single chapter in books dedicated to broader topics such as general ethics, bioethics, marriage, or love. Most studies of contraception and the Orthodox tradition also exhibit a paucity of references to primary sources, often relying on broad generalizations rather than sustained examination of the patristic and ecclesiastical tradition in order to draw their conclusions.

The present study therefore seeks to offer a more probing examination of the Orthodox moral tradition as it pertains to contraception. In treating this subject, it limits itself to the issue noted above, namely, contraception understood as the stifling, nullification, or destruction of the natural fecundity *of the marital act* as such. This includes barrier methods and other technological and pharmaceutical interventions that render the sex act infertile by human intervention or obstruction. By focusing on acts and means intended to divorce sexual intercourse from the conception of children, it leaves aside the larger question of whether it is morally licit to avoid childbearing in general, for example through the use of periodic or strategic abstinence. Although such practices could be defined as contraceptive in a broad sense, they differ from the moral act involved in impeding or suppressing the natural consequences of insemination. For these reasons, this study does not deal directly with the wider questions surrounding infertility and natural family planning. Those questions, while important, are separated for the time being.

In reviewing and studying the evidence, this study seeks to demonstrate that the Orthodox Church has not been nearly so silent on the issue of contraception as is sometimes thought. In addition to offering clear moral principles with clear ramifications for Christian marriage and conjugal love, the Orthodox tradition speaks with a consistent voice about the impropriety of contraception, even if this component of the ethical tradition has not been as relevant in times past as it is today. If there remains a need in the twenty-first century to highlight or emphasize the traditional Orthodox opposition to contraception in light of our changed circumstances, then it may be time for pastors, teachers, and all who preach the Gospel to bring this patrimony to bear more explicitly on the needs of today's flock. The goal, however, is not to lay heavy burdens on men's shoulders (Mt 23:4), but to help the Orthodox faithful *walk in the Spirit* along the narrow path of a fully Orthodox Christian ethic.[6]

---

[6] See Romans 8:1, 4; Galatians 5:16, 25; Ephesians 2:2.

Approaching the Issue from an Orthodox Perspective

Any assessment of ethical issues, as with all issues relating to Christian life and praxis, must, in the context of Orthodox Christian theology, have its roots in a tradition that is professed to be both ancient and unchanging. Deacon Perry Hamalis, a researcher and author in Orthodox ethics, refers in this sense to "Orthodoxy's universal and ancient ethical teaching."[7] As Orthodox Christians, we look for truth, in all matters, within a patrimony that is now nearly two thousand years old. This is because Orthodox Christians believe that piety (*eusebeia*), in both its ethical and dogmatic dimensions, was not only delivered once and for all by Christ Himself through the apostles, but is also preserved and transmitted in the Church throughout the ages. Our faith, according to the formula of St Athanasius the Great, is "what Christ bestowed, what the apostles preached, and what the Fathers handed down."[8]

---

[7] Perry T. Hamalis, "Orthodoxy and Bioethics," in J. McGuckin, ed., *The Encyclopedia of Eastern Orthodox Christianity*, vol. 1 (West Sussex: Blackwell, 2011), 575.

[8] To the Bishops of Africa, 1: ἣν ὁ μὲν Χριστὸς ἐχαρίσατο, οἱ δὲ ἀπόστολοι ἐκήρυξαν, καὶ οἱ Πατέρες παραδεδώκασιν (PG 26:1029A). Cf. *To Serapion* 1.28.1: "Let us look ... to that tradition (παράδοσιν), teaching, and faith of the Catholic Church that is from the beginning, which the Lord gave, the apostles

This God-preserved transmission by those whom we call our Fathers is the reason that the mind of the Church is equated, in the Orthodox context, with *patristic* tradition. St Symeon of Thessalonica, writing in the fifteenth century, explains,

No one knows the things of man except the spirit that is in him, and no one knows the things of God except the Spirit that is in Him (1 Cor 2:11). Who then will boast that he understands what is loftier than the Spirit? The Fathers, however, and what is contained in the divine Scriptures, are of the Spirit.... Who, then, would in any way dare to act contemptuously towards the Scriptures, or to say anything contrary to the Spirit-bearing Fathers?... The Lord, also, beginning from Moses and from all the prophets, interpreted in all the Scriptures what was written about Him (Lk 24:27). And none of the apostles and Fathers failed to bear witness to this teaching to the faithful. Who, then, would dare to put forward another faith contrary to the Scriptures and contrary to the Fathers who possess the Spirit, or to negate the faith revealed through the Spirit to the Fathers?[9]

---

preached, and the Fathers safeguarded (ἐφύλαξαν). For on this the Church was founded, and whoever falls from it is no longer, and should no longer be called, a Christian" (ed. Kyriakos Savvidis, *Athanasius Werke* 1.1.4: Epistulae I–IV ad Serapionem [Berlin: De Gruyter, 2010], 519–520).

[9] *Dialogue in Christ 23* (PG 155:121D–124A), trans. T. Pino, *St Symeon of Thessalonica: Against All Heresies* (Riverside, CA: Patristic Nectar Publications, 2023), 157.

The fundamentally patristic character of Orthodox piety ensures that ethical debates and questions are not relegated to the realm of relativity or deemed unknowable and elusive, since every voice on the subject is necessarily and admittedly appealing to the same sources. Yet to profess that the tradition of the Church acts as an unchanging guide even on questions of morality is not to say that our historical and external circumstances do not change, or that the contingencies of human life do not demand new applications and contemporary interpretations. On this, every Orthodox Christian can agree. As William Basil Zion puts it, "It is not enough to repeat the opinion and teachings of the Fathers of the Church. These teachings must be interpreted by the Church in each generation."[10]

To a certain extent, the ongoing need to appropriate the apostolic tradition in every age means that the continuing life of the Church, and the present pastoral responsibilities of hierarchs, must often fulfill what is lacking in the tradition (cf. Col 1:24), not because the doctrines of the Church are incomplete or lacking in themselves, but because every set of circumstances and conditions requires a living application of the timeless tradition. This, in its most fundamental sense, is what is meant by *oeconomia*: the exercise of a

---

[10] William Basil Zion, *Eros and Transformation* (Lanham, MD: University Press of America, 1992), 242.

judicious household management that brings forth out of the patristic treasury things new and old (Mt 13:52). Whether one is 'conservative' or 'liberal,' this means that we do not limit ourselves merely to the letter of the law as regards patristic tradition. In the words of Fr Seraphim Rose,

> Our attitude to the Fathers must be more serious and more profound than this. Being faithful to the Fathers does not mean merely being ready to quote them or feel 'free' to think as one pleases if no quotes are available. Rather, it means entering into their thought, which is the thought of the Church of Christ, and having a coherent philosophy of life derived from our life in the Church in harmony with the thought of the Fathers.[11]

Deacon Perry Hamalis echoes this sentiment when he notes, "Orthodox bioethicists must strive to 'acquire the mind of the church' so as to relate Orthodoxy's universal and ancient ethical teaching to the particular and new situations confronted today."[12]

---

[11] Fr Seraphim Rose, *Genesis, Creation, and Early Man*, 2nd ed. (Platina, CA: St. Herman Press, 2011), 511.
[12] Perry Hamalis, "Orthodoxy and Bioethics," 575. Cf. Chrysostom Zaphiris, "Morality of Contraception: An Eastern Orthodox Opinion," *Journal of Ecumenical Studies* 11.4 (Fall 1974): 677–90 (677).

In approaching the issue of contraception, therefore, we must examine not only what the Fathers have to say, but whether our contemporary modes of thinking are in keeping with the mind of the Church throughout the ages. We begin our assessment, then, with an examination of where we stand today in relation to the Church's "universal and ancient ethical teaching."

A New Consensus

It is acutely obvious today that many Orthodox Christians, both among the laity and the clergy, have come to accept contraception as an unquestioned part of contemporary life. Even in the absence of real statistics, it is plain that contraception is not a controversial issue for most Orthodox, either at the personal level, in ordinary parishes, or within the synods of local churches. Though one certainly finds bishops, priests, and monastic communities that advocate abstention from contraceptives,[13] this is not an issue that characterizes

---

[13] A popular "Preparation for Holy Confession" that circulates in certain monasteries, parishes, and on the internet, asks, as part of its examination of conscience, "[D]o you prevent yourself from having children (i.e. contraception)?" The pamphlet, however, while widely used, is not so common as to be considered normative in modern Orthodox life. See, also, below, p. 25 nn. 31–35.

modern Orthodox preaching the way that it character-izes, for example, the official position of the Roman Catholic Church.[14] In this respect the practice of Ortho-dox Christians has, by and large, kept pace with trends in secular society. As contraception has become nor-malized in society at large, so it has become ordinary and accepted within the Orthodox Church.[15]

Orthodox Christians, however, have also, in char-acteristic fashion, been somewhat behind the times. The gradual acceptance of contraception at a pastoral and personal level only began to materialize among Orthodox populations in the 1960s and 70s, approxi-mately thirty to forty years after it was first admitted by the Anglican Church. The gradual and palpable shift is famously on display in successive editions of *The Orthodox Church* by Metropolitan Kallistos Ware. Writing in 1963, as Timothy Ware, the future Metro-politan stated unequivocally that,

> Artificial methods of birth control are forbid-den in the Orthodox Church.[16]

---

[14] See the *Catechism of the Catholic Church*, nos. 2399 and 2370.

[15] For a sobering look at how social taboos and attitudes towards contraception have functioned in a place like Greece, see Violetta Hionidou, *Abortion and Contraception in Modern Greece, 1830–1967: Medicine, Sexuality and Popular Culture* (Newcastle: Palgrave Macmillan, 2020).

[16] Ware, *The Orthodox Church* (London: Penguin, 1963), 302.

Twenty years later, this statement would be adjusted to account for changes that were then in the air:

> Some bishops and theologians altogether condemn the employment of [artificial methods of birth control]. Others, however, have recently begun to adopt a less strict position.[17]

A decade later, bishop Kallistos narrates the end of the process:

> In the past birth control was in general strongly condemned, but today a less strict view is coming to prevail.[18]

In these successive revisions to his book, the late Metropolitan Kallistos traces the development of a new consensus that moved from complete condemnation in 1963—which is to say, over the course of nearly two thousand years of Church history—to near total acceptance in less than fifty years. Today, the "less strict view" is more than prevalent. It in fact constitutes the status quo for hundreds of thousands of members of the Orthodox Church, raising obvious issues about the continuity of Orthodox Christian moral teaching.

---

[17] Ware, *The Orthodox Church* (London: Penguin, 1984), 302.
[18] Ware, *The Orthodox Church* (London: Penguin, 1993), 296.

Although Metropolitan Kallistos speaks only of a position held by "some bishops and theologians," and of a "view" that has come to prevail, the implications for Orthodox theology are obvious. Over the past several decades, therefore, it has not been uncommon for commentators both inside and outside the Church to equate the new status quo and the updated consensus among pastors and theologians with the actual teaching of the Orthodox Church. Some theologians and ethicists have therefore spoken boldly of a *change* in Orthodox doctrine. Fr Stanley Harakas, for example, speaks in this context of an "exception to the [Church's] continuity of teaching."[19] Basilio Petrà, too, a Roman Catholic priest, ethicist, and theologian, expresses a familiar position when he celebrates what he sees as the volte-face of Orthodox theology, ascribed to the laudable flexibility and pastoral condescension of the Orthodox.[20]

Does this novel status quo, however, express the 'official' teaching of the Orthodox Church? If the

---

[19] Stanley Harakas, "The Stand of the Orthodox Church on Controversial Issues," https://www.goarch.org/-/the-stand-of-the-orthodox-church-on-controversial-issues, accessed 31 December 2023.

[20] Basilio Petrà: *La contraccezione nella tradizione ortodossa. Forza della realtà e mediazione pastorale* (Firenze: Edizione Dehoniane Bologna, 2009). Like Ware, Petrà explains that the Orthodox Church, prior to recent decades, consistently opposed contraception; see, esp., pp. 40–41, 48–53.

attitude towards contraception in certain circles has followed in lockstep with popular culture, to what extent does this express the mind of the Church, to say nothing of the explicit teaching of the Fathers?

Searching for the 'Official' Voice of the Church

It is sometimes argued that no ecumenical council or 'official' magisterial source has ever promulgated a teaching on the subject of contraception. In the words of Fr John Meyendorff, "The Orthodox Church, for its part, has never committed itself formally and officially on this issue."[21] As ambiguous and potentially misleading as such a statement may be, it is nonetheless true that nothing in the order of the Lambeth Conferences of the Anglican Communion or the papal encyclicals and *Catechism* of the Roman Catholic Church has ever articulated a definitive and up-to-date position for or against contraception in the Orthodox Church. Nevertheless, this is not, as we shall see, an indication of the

---

[21]John Meyendorff, *Marriage: An Orthodox Perspective* (Crestwood: St. Vladimir's Seminary Press, 1984), 61. Cf. Zaphiris, "Morality of Contraception," 681; John McGuckin, *The Orthodox Church: An Introduction to its History, Doctrine, and Spiritual Culture* (Malden, MA: Blackwell, 2008), 312.

Church's silence or ambivalence on the topic. Ecclesiastical doctrine and the tradition of the Fathers can certainly not be reduced to the decrees of ecumenical councils or the Orthodox equivalent of papal encyclicals (whatever those might be). This would be an oversimplification and reduction of the Church's tradition that would leave us with little that we commonly recognize as Orthodox.

In the context of the modern debate over contraception, the Holy Synod of the Church of Greece was among the first ecclesial bodies to respond to the global controversy impacting American and European society in the early twentieth century. In 1937, the Synod issued an encyclical letter responding to the prominent trend of the 1920s and 30s known as neo-Malthusianism. This movement, which derives its name from Thomas Robert Malthus (1766–1834) and his concerns regarding overpopulation and eugenics, lay at the heart of the contraception movement that dominated scientific and political discussions of that era. Under the presidency of Chrysostomos II of Athens, the Hierarchy of the Church of Greece, represented by its fifty-six signatories, in an encyclical *To the Sacred Clergy and Pious People of Greece*, therefore decried "the obstruction of the conception of children" as a manifestation of the same "genocidal evil" that gave rise to the sin of abortion.[22] Citing Walter Lippmann, it called contraception a crime and "the most revolutionary practice in the history of morals."[23] Though the bishops expressed their sensitivity to the real challenges of family life, they called on couples to embrace an authentic and fundamentally ascetical Christian life, rejecting all forms of contraception, which only served to distort the nuptial mystery:

> We are not unaware of that category of parents who are faced with great difficulties in their married life, either because they bear unsustainable financial burdens or because

[22] Hierarchy of the Church of Greece, "Encyclical of 1937: To the Sacred Clergy and Pious People of Greece," *Ekklesia* 42 (23 October 1937): 329–333. This text is associated with Fr Seraphim Papakostas, founder of the Zoe movement. Papakostas opposed contraception in his *Το ζήτημα της τεκνογονίας* (Athens: Zoe Brotherhood, 1933; revised 1947). For one response to the encyclical, see Alexandros M. Stavropoulos, *Το πρόβλημα της τεκνογονίας και η Εγκύκλιος της Εκκλησίας της Ελλάδος* (1937). *Συμβολή εις την Ποιμαντικήν της Τεκνογονίας εξ επόψεως ορθοδόξου* (Athens: s.n., 1977). For discussion of the role of the Church within the debate over contraception in Greece, see Hionidou, *Abortion and Contraception in Modern Greece*, 181–183; Petrà, *La contracezzione*, 48–117.

[23] "Encyclical of 1937," 329 (§ 4). See the translation below, pp. 90–91. Walter Lippmann (1889–1974) was a prominent journalist, cultural commentator, and the winner of two Pulitzer Prizes. He was an ardent critic of birth control, especially from 1927 to 1929.

childbearing entails a direct danger to the life of the mother. We nurture deep compassion for them. We appeal to them, however, to bear in mind that in the life of a family, as in the life of every individual, we are called to carry a cross and to suffer trials. But we must put all our hope in the power of God, who enables us to bear the weight of our cross. In these circumstances spouses have a duty to abstain, as they do in the circumstances indicated by the Apostle Paul, when he spoke of the temporary abstinence of spouses for the sake of fasting and prayer (1 Cor 7:1–6). Abstinence constitutes for spouses the only lawful means of avoiding childbearing when a real need for it is present.[24]

If the bearing of children had to be avoided, the Synod concluded, this could only be effected through self-restraint and not through the artificial separation of sexual intercourse from its natural procreative capacity.

Later, in 1978, at a time when the nation of Greece was considering the legalization of abortion, the Holy Synod re-affirmed its Encyclical of 1937, citing "an imperative need to repeat this recommendation again today and to renew through this present proclamation what

---

[24] "Encyclical of 1937," 332 (§ 22). See the translation below, pp. 103.

our Mother, the Church, proclaimed to her children forty years ago."[25] The 1978 Encyclical, *To All the People of Greece*, included the same appeal for each Christian "to take up and bear his cross, just as the Lord himself did, and not to renounce his fundamental duties."[26] Though the message contains evidence that Church members were seeking dispensations and *oeconomia* on the issue of contraception, the encyclical states that the bishops were not able to bless an alternative to conjugal abstinence in those cases when pregnancy must be avoided:

> The Holy Synod of the Hierarchy is not unaware that there are also difficult circumstances and problematic, and sometimes dangerous, situations in the matter of childbearing and childrearing. Either for financial reasons or because of living conditions, etc.—even for reasons of health—it is not a simple matter, and often acute problems arise. In order to deal with these difficulties, many are seeking a way out. Yet the only acceptable way out for a Christian, through conjugal abstinence, is usually seen as a strait gate and a narrow way (Mt 7:14) and a heavy and unbearable burden.

---

[25] Hierarchy of the Church of Greece, "Encyclical of 1978: To All the People of Greece," *Ekklesia* 22–23 (1978): 563–564; 563 (§5). See the translation below, p. 108.

[26] "Encyclical of 1978," 563 (§10). See the translation below, p. 109.

It is, for the majority of people, something unattainable, and *few are those who find it* (that is, the way). For this reason, some further dispensation and 'ecclesiastical economy' and condescension is being sought for and deemed desirable.... [Nevertheless] the Holy Synod of the Hierarchy cannot take up a decision that is contrary to the sacred Canons regarding the exercise of 'ecclesiastical economy' as many are requesting for particular special cases.[27]

In this way, the Church of Greece expressed in 1978 what was considered in 1937 to be the unchanging tradition of the Church. As the bishops expressed it in their first encyclical,

[T]he tradition of the Church is consistent and has been passed on to us unchanged from the times of the apostles. It teaches that the avoidance of children is a lawless act and a deliberate resistance by man to the will of God. If, in this matter, even heterodox Churches have tried not to deviate from this tradition, all the more is faithful adherence incumbent upon us the Orthodox, the unbending custodians of the dogmatic and moral truths handed down to us from the beginning.[28]

---

[27] "Encyclical of 1978," 564 (§17–18, §20). See the translation below, pp. 111–112.
[28] "Encyclical of 1937," 332 (§17). See the translation below, p. 100.

The Church of Romania is reported to have issued a similar rejection of birth control, though this might simply be a reference to the nationwide ban on contraceptives imposed in Romania beginning in 1966, a measure likely supported by the Church.[29] Nevertheless, in its 1997 *Pastoral Message (Cuvântul Pastoral)*, the Holy Synod of the Romanian Orthodox Church included contraception alongside abortion as a sin and a "violation of nature" with "serious and painful consequences."[30]

In both Greece and Romania, the practice of contraception has continued to be opposed by modern saints, elders, confessors, and spiritual writers. The recently canonized St Porphyrios of Kafsokalyvia declares in this spirit that, "Avoiding childbearing is not allowed. It is a great sin!"[31] Similar views

---

[29] See Demetrios J. Constantelos, *Marriage, Sexuality, and Celibacy: A Greek Orthodox Perspective* (Minneapolis: Light and Life Publishing, 1975), 37; cf. Petrà, *La contraccezione*, 42 n. 51. Ceaușescu banned both abortion and contraception in his infamous Decree 770.

[30] *Buletinul Oficiel al Patriarhiei Române* 115.106 (January–June 1997), 13: "Nu numai avortul, dar și contracepția, au urmări grave și dureroase. Violarea legilor naturale, așezate de Dumnezeu, prin practici anticoncepționale presupune și expunerea la sancțiuni ulterioare."

[31] Kleitos Ioannides, *Ο Γέρων Πορφύριος: Μαρτυρίες και Εμπειρίες* [*Elder Porphyrios: Testimonies and Experiences*] (Athens: Transfiguration of the Savior Monastery, 1997), 135; cited in Engelhardt, *Foundations of Christian Bioethics*, 267). Patriarch Irinej of Serbia, in his 2018 Christmas interview with

are expressed by Metropolitan Augoustinos of Florina (d. 2010),[32] Fr Arsenie Boca (d. 1989),[33] Fr Arsenie Papacioc (d. 2011),[34] and Fr Nicolae Tănase.[35]

 The position of the Russian Church in recent times has been less clear. Contraception and the avoidance of childbearing was long looked upon with disdain in Russian Orthodox culture, and to this day it continues to be rejected among the Old Believers.[36] Yet this position has not been as clearly maintained by the modern Russian Orthodox Church. In the year 2000, at the Jubilee Council of Bishops, the Moscow Patriarchate

---

'Телевизија Храм,' likewise advocated for the bearing of many children and noted that it would have been "unthinkable" just a few decades ago to teach children about contraception (https://www.tvhram.rs/emisije/517/intervju-patrijarha-irineja-susret-bozicu-januar, accessed 31 December 2023).

[32] See *Metropolitan Augoustinos N. Kantiotes: A Short Biography*, trans. Alexander Filip (Paros: Zoodochos Pigi Monastery, 2015), 137.

[33] See Arsenie Boca, *Tinerii, familia şi copii născuţi în lanţuri* (Iaşi: Editura Credinţa strămoşească, 2005), 33.

[34] See Benedict Stancu, ed., *Iată duhovnicul: părintele Arsenie Papacioc*, vol. 2 (Bucharest: Editura Sophia, 2006), 62.

[35] See Nicolae Tănase, *Soţul ideal, soţia ideală* (Sibiu: Editura Anastasis, 2011), 26.

[36] In addition to the pervasive evidence for this at a pastoral level, see the research of Alla Makarentseva, "Семья и рождение детей в жизненном пути старообрядцев [Family and Childbearing in the Life Course of the Old Believers]," *Государство, религия, церковь в России и за рубежом [State, Religion, and Church in Russia and Abroad]* 40.4 (2022): 139–162.

published a set of guidelines for its clergy dealing with various social issues facing Christians today: the so-called *Basis of the Social Concept of the Russian Orthodox Church*. This document states that, "Among the problems which need a religious and moral assessment is that of contraception." Like the *Catechism of the Catholic Church*, it acknowledges the need for couples to bear the office of parenthood responsibly. It nevertheless distinguishes between abortifacient and non-abortifacient contraceptives, stating that, "Christian spouses should remember that human reproduction is one of the principal purposes of the divinely established marital union. The deliberate refusal of childbirth on egoistic grounds devalues marriage and is a definite sin."[37]

The distinction between abortifacient and non-abortifacient contraceptives, as well as the qualification "on egoistic grounds" could perhaps be seen to imply that contraception admits of a permissible use. To the extent that certain forms of contraception do not consist in the destruction of a fertilized embryo, and because couples may seek to avoid pregnancy for non-egoistic reasons (such as medical necessity), it would seem to be implied that there are occasions in

---

[37] "Basis of the Social Concept of the Russian Orthodox Church" 12.3, https://old.mospat.ru/en/documents/social-concepts/, accessed 31 December 2023.

which contraception is not sinful or evil, contrary to what was expressed in previous centuries. This implication would seem to be compounded by the call to *responsible* parenthood and the subsequent discussion of abstinence as a potential means for effecting it: "[S]pouses are responsible before God for the comprehensive upbringing of their children. One of the ways to be responsible for their birth is to restrain themselves from sexual relations for a time."[38]

The *Social Concept* document subsequently urges caution on clergy in imposing this ascesis:

> Clearly, spouses should make such decisions mutually on the counsel of their spiritual father. The latter should take into account, with pastoral prudence, the concrete living conditions of the couple, their age, health, degree of spiritual maturity and many other circumstances. In doing so, he should distinguish those who can hold the high demands of continence from those to whom it is not given (Mt. 19:11), taking care above all the preservation and consolidation of the family.[39]

---

[38] "Basis of the Social Concept of the Russian Orthodox Church," 12.3.

[39] "Basis of the Social Concept of the Russian Orthodox Church," 12.3.

With these provisions, the *Social Concept* document has seemed to some to seal the interpretation that the Moscow Patriarchate has therefore conditionally allowed birth control.[40]

Yet it is significant that the synodal statement itself does not take this step outright, exercising as much caution against openly permitting the use of contraception as it does against being entirely insensitive to pastoral conditions. Indeed, several of its implications can be read in different ways. To acknowledge the existence, for example, of non-egoistic motivations for avoiding childbirth is not the same as license to do so by any means. The 1937 Encyclical of the Church of Greece in fact makes a similar claim. "We adamantly protest," it says, "and absolutely condemn every method of neo-Malthusianism, which defiles the purity of family life and thwarts conception for selfish reasons, for comforts, and for luxuries."[41] Yet the same encyclical is also unequivocal that "in especially difficult circumstances, when the avoidance of childbearing is unavoidably imposed, the only lawful recourse is abstinence from conjugal relations by means of self-restraint."[42] Much the same could be said for the call to

---

[40] See John W. Morris, *The Historic Church: An Orthodox View of Christian History* (Bloomington, IN: AuthorHouse Publishing, 2011), 217.

[41] "Encyclical of 1937," 332 (§21).

[42] "Encyclical of 1937," 331 (§13).

responsible childbearing. Yet, whatever its implications, and whatever arguments from silence might be brought forward against it, the *Basis for the Social Concept of the Russian Orthodox Church* actually remains silent, if a bit ambiguous, on the permissibility of contraception. As such, even if it fails to articulate or address the Church's historical opposition to contraception, this text from the modern Moscow Patriarchate also does not take the step of officially endorsing artificial birth control.

Much more explicit, and problematic, are the 1992 *Synodal Affirmations on Marriage, Family, Sexuality, and the Sanctity of Life* issued by the Synod of Bishops of the Orthodox Church in America (OCA) at their tenth All-American Council. This document explicitly states,

> Married couples may express their love in sexual union without always intending the conception of a child, but only those means of controlling conception within marriage are acceptable which do not harm a fetus already conceived.[43]

Though couched in language that is aimed at repudiating abortifacients, this affirmation by the Holy

---

[43] Holy Synod of Bishops, "Synodal Affirmations on Marriage, Family, Sexuality, and the Sanctity of Life," https://www.oca.org/holy-synod/statements/holy-synod/synodal-affirmations-on-marriage-family-sexuality-and-the-sanctity-of-life, accessed 31 December 2023.

Synod of the OCA is remarkable for its proclamation that non-abortifacient forms of contraception "are acceptable." The text thereby makes explicit what is perhaps merely implied by the Moscow Patriarchate's *Social Concept* document and thus expresses for the first time in an official ecclesiastical document the novel status quo described by Kallistos Ware as "coming to prevail" in the 1980s and 90s. The *Synodal Affirmations* therefore constitute what is perhaps the first 'official' statement in the history of the Church to explicitly condone contraception.

Needless to say, the 1992 *Synodal Affirmations* of the OCA Synod offer no rationale for the adoption of this change in moral outlook. Neither the document nor any subsequent declarations present any evidence as to why what was once unacceptable is acceptable today. Nor, in expressing what is undoubtedly a novel approval for contraception, do these *Synodal Affirmations* make any effort to ground their approbation in patristic sources or in the tradition of the Church.

More than thirty years have now passed since the *Synodal Affirmations* of the OCA were first published in 1992. In this time, the popular acceptance of contraception has not waned. On the contrary, Orthodox Christians have only become more entrenched in the assumption that contraception is an acceptable part of conjugal life. More recently, this truism has been repeated in another 'official' document, this one commissioned by the Ecumenical Patriarchate of Constantinople. Following the Great and Holy Synod of 2016, the Ecumenical Patriarchate organized and endorsed the composition of its own social document addressing contemporary issues: *For the Life of the World: Towards a Social Ethos of the Orthodox Church.* This document, drafted by a twelve-person committee of mostly anglophone scholars, was released in 2020.[44] It confidently affirms ,

> The Church anticipates, of course, that most marriages will be open to conception; but it also understands that there are situations in which spiritual, physical, psychological, or financial impediments arise that make it wise—at least, for a time—to delay or forego the bearing of children. The Orthodox Church has no dogmatic objection to the use of safe and non-abortifacient contraceptives within the context of married life, not as an ideal or as a permanent arrangement, but as a provisional concession to necessity.[45]

[44] The Special Commission consisted of John Chryssavgis, David Bentley Hart, George Demacopoulos, Carrie Frederick Frost, Brandon Gallaher, Perry Hamalis, Nicolas Kazarian, Aristotle Papanikolaou, James Skedros, Gayle Woloschak, Konstantinos Delikostantis, and Theodoros Yiangou.

[45] *For the Life of the World: Towards a Social Ethos of the Orthodox Church,* 24, https://www.goarch.org/social-ethos, accessed 31 December 2023.

With these claims, the document entitled *For the Life of the World* purports to speak for the Church in the most definitive of terms. Gesturing towards the limited role that contraception should play in a Christian marriage, it nevertheless expands the conditions in which contraception may be used. Noting that "most," though not all, marriages should be open to the bearing of children, it adds spiritual and psychological impediments to the list of reasons that married couples might lawfully obstruct conception during sexual intercourse. Yet, once again, the document offers no argumentation or explanation as to how this new consensus of the twentieth century accurately represents "the social doctrine of the Orthodox Church, as this has been reflected and expressed in the tradition through the centuries."[46]

If the widespread acceptance of contraception is indeed a new phenomenon, as it is both in the secular world and in the Church, then it is necessary to explain why the public position has changed. Whereas the Orthodox Church condemned contraception well into the second half of the twentieth century, some modern voices, even rising to the level of synodal and patriarchal documents, have very clearly reversed course. Why

[46] *For the Life of the World: Towards a Social Ethos of the Orthodox Church*, Preface (authored by John Chryssavgis and David Bentley Hart).

has this occurred? If, as Kallistos Ware and the Hierarchy of the Church of Greece declared, the Church condemned birth control continuously for two millennia, what has changed? Before we examine the thinking of the modern scholars who set this change in motion, let us turn to some of the ancient and medieval sources of the ecclesiastical tradition to see where the Church's historical position originated.

Contraception and the Ancient Church

Orthodox theology, as already noted, looks for its understanding of apostolic tradition in the Fathers of the Church: those voices that maintained and perpetuated, in the Spirit, the *paradosis* of Christ himself. Yet on the subject of contraception, it is sometimes asserted that the Fathers do not address the issue, or have nothing to say on the subject, since it is an entirely modern phenomenon. Paul Evdokimov, for example, makes the sweeping claim that, "In the age of the Church Fathers, the problem of birth control was never raised.... One must therefore start from the *patristic spirit* and not from a precise, inexistent teaching."[47]

---

[47] Paul Evdokimov, *The Sacrament of Love* (Crestwood: St Vladimir's Seminary Press, 1985), 174; emphasis in the original.

The idea, however, that the issue of contraception was never countenanced "in the age of the Church Fathers" is not difficult to disprove. Leaving aside the question of a patristic 'age,' which limits the existence of divinely inspired teachers and saints to antiquity, it is nevertheless untrue that contraception is a uniquely modern phenomenon. Whereas modern technologies and the transformation of social mores have certainly created an unprecedented ethical and pastoral challenge for modern Orthodox Christians, the practice of contraception, and even the existence of contraceptive devices, methods, and chemical interventions is by no means new.

Contraception, as already outlined above, refers, for the purposes of this study, to the deliberate obstruction of conception during the marital act. It includes any method or means of interference that destroys the natural fecundity of conjugal intercourse and interferes with or seeks to disrupt the natural consequences of insemination. In Western civilization, the classic and most basic example of such behavior is the story of Onan in the book of Genesis (Gen 38:4–10). Onan, the son of Judah and grandson of the patriarch Jacob, is said to have used coitus interruptus to prevent the impregnation of his dead brother's wife, Tamar.

> And Judah took a wife for Er his firstborn, whose name was Tamar. And it happened that

Er, the firstborn of Judah, was wicked in the sight of the Lord, and the Lord slew him. And Judah said unto Onan, "Go in unto thy brother's wife, and marry her, and raise up seed to thy brother." And Onan knew that the seed (τὸ σπέρμα) should not be his; and it came to pass, when he went in unto his brother's wife, that he spilled it (ἐξέχεεν) on the ground, lest he should give seed to his brother. And the thing that he did was wicked in the sight of God, and he slew him also.[48]

The story of Onan has long been identified both with the avoidance of conception through coitus interruptus and with auto-erotic self-abuse, to which it has given the name 'Onanism.'[49] Paul Evdokimov, however, asserts that to interpret the story of Onan as a repudiation of contraception is "an exegetical blunder."[50] The context of Evdokimov's declaration is his response to *Casti Connubii*, in which the Roman Catholic Church states that it is,

Small wonder, therefore, if Holy Writ bears witness that the Divine Majesty regards with greatest detestation this horrible crime

---

[48] Genesis 38:6–10, LXX.

[49] See, for example, the *Oxford English Dictionary*, s.v. "Onanism."

[50] Evdokimov, *The Sacrament of Love*, 174.

[namely, contraception] and at times has pun-
ished it with death. As St. Augustine notes,
"Intercourse even with one's legitimate wife
is unlawful and wicked where the conception
of the offspring is prevented. Onan, the son of
Juda, did this and the Lord killed him for it."[51]

For Evdokimov, this is nothing but facile moral-
izing that fails to appreciate the accurate meaning of
the biblical text. The fact that it is the interpretation of
St Augustine also does little to recommend the position. Other writers, like William Basil Zion, insist that
the sin of Onan was not the spilling of his seed as such
(and thus his distortion of the marital act by preventing conception), but his failure to fulfill the law of levi-
rate, whereby a man has the duty to raise up offspring
for his dead brother (see Deut 25:5–10).

Zion's position, which is prevalent among scholars today, is predicated on the assumption that modern
historical criticism has given us a superior understanding of the Scriptures than what was available to ancient
and medieval authors.[52] Yet it is not only St Augustine

---

[51] Pope Pius XI, I, Casti Connubii (31 December 1930), par. 55,
citing St Augustine, *On Adulterous Marriages* 2.12.

[52] Zion, *Eros and Transformation*, 240. The idea that we
now understand the Onan account better because of new or
improved access to the Hebrew version is belied by Rabbinic
interpretation. One modern Midrashic exegesis says of Onan

who identifies the crime of Onan with the unlawful avoidance of fecundation during sex. This is also the interpretation of Saints Jerome and Epiphanius.

Jerome, a scholar of Semitic languages and bridge between the Greek and Latin traditions, clearly sees Onan's exercise of coitus interruptus as immoral in itself. Onan, Jerome notes, "was killed because he begrudged his brother seed." The reason, he explains, is specifically connected to his distortion of the sexual act. Speaking rhetorically about the fact that the Bible contains instances of immoral behavior, so that not everything that is found in Scripture is set before us as an example, Jerome notes that the case of Onan is included in Scripture, "as if we approved of any sort of emission of seed except for the procreation of children (*qualemcumque seminis fluxum absque liberorum opere*).[53]

St Epiphanius of Cyprus, himself an influence on St. Jerome, holds the same view. Speaking in his *Refutation of All Heresies* about the fourth-century

---

that, "He misused the organs God gave him for propagating the race to unnaturally satisfy his own lust, and he was therefore deserving of death" (*Bereshis: Genesis—A New Translation with a Commentary Authorized from Talmudic, Midrashic and Rabbinic Sources* [Brooklyn: Mesorah Publications, 1980], 1677).

[53] *Against Jovinian* 1.20 (PL 23:249A).

Gnostics, Epiphanius explains that in their disdain for procreation, they promote forms of intercourse and sexual gratification that consciously avoid fecundation, thereby imitating the crime of Onan:

> They say that virgins are those women who in the worldly commingling of natural marital intercourse have never gone so far as to be inseminated (ἕως καταβολῆς σπέρματος). Yet these women still come together with men all the time and commit fornication. Nevertheless, before the consummation of their pleasure, they cause the wicked perpetrator of their union to withdraw and then consume the aforementioned shame [that is, the human seed] as food, after the manner of [Onan's] malfeasance toward Tamar. In place of virginity they have substituted this method of defiling themselves, without, however, accepting the commingling and insemination (ἀπόρροιαν) of the defilement.[54]

We shall return to Epiphanius's description of Gnostic practices below. Yet whatever the sensibilities

---

[54] *Panarion* 26.11.10–11, ed. Karl Holl, *Epiphanius (Ancoratus und Panarion)*, vol. 1, Die griechischen christlichen Schriftsteller [GCS] 25 (Leipzig: Hinrichs, 1915), 290. The text attributes the crime to Shelah (see Gen 38:11), but the reference is to the action of Onan at 38:9; see below, 48 n. 85.

of the Church Fathers may have been to the story of Onan, and however much those sensibilities might differ from our own, it is clear that patristic biblical exegesis touches explicitly on the central question surrounding contraception: the ruination of fertilization and the obstruction of impregnation during intercourse. It is therefore untrue on its face that the problem of suppressing conception was "never raised" in the ancient Church. Indeed, it is apparent that "the patristic spirit" was closely concerned with precisely the ethical issues presently under discussion.

Impeding Conception in the Early Church

In addition to contraceptive methods and techniques like coitus interruptus, contraceptive applications, medicines, and devices were also a common feature of pre-modern life. In his magisterial study entitled *Contraception: A History of Its Treatment by the Catholic Theologians and Canonists*, John T. Noonan, provides a substantive overview of this age-old practice from ancient Egypt through the High Middle Ages as background for examining the modern Roman Catholic doctrine on birth control. Noonan, who himself served on the papal commission that recommended *relaxing*

the ban on contraception, was by no means an apologist for the strict papal position. Yet his monograph
articulates, in compelling detail, how later Christian
opposition, in the modern context, relates to centu-
ries-old practices and ideas.[55]

Noonan is by no means original in his research
on this question. As he states in the first chapter of
his book, "The existence of contraceptive technique in
the pre-Christian Mediterranean world is well established."[56] From the application of pulverized crocodile
dung to the use of wool suppositories, human beings
of days gone by were no less desirous of disconnect-
ing sexual activity from the conception of children than
human beings today. Indeed, the desire to uncouple
sexual pleasure from its dramatic consequences might
have been felt even more urgently prior to the advent
of modern medicine, when the risk of death, disease,
and other forms of suffering were felt somewhat more
acutely. Yet regardless of the motivation, it is clear, as
John Riddle explains, that, "From the British Isles to
the eastern Mediterranean, late antiquity and the early
Middle Ages knew about antifertility measures both

---

[55] John T. Noonan, *Contraception: A History of Its Treatment by the Catholic Theologians and Canonists*, Enlarged Edition (Cambridge, MA: Harvard University Press, 1986).
[56] Noonan, *Contraception*, 9.

from classical texts and from their own contributors."[57] The Church Fathers, and the wider Christian world, were no exception.

The use of contraceptives, which divorce sexual activity from the conception of children, is often associated in Christian texts with adultery and fornication, a context in which children are obviously unwanted. St Hippolytus of Rome, an important theological writer and martyr of the third century, thus criticizes the hypocrisy of noble Roman women, whom he calls Christian in name alone, for their use of contraceptive remedies. "The so-called faithful," he says, "use anti-pregnancy medications (ἀτοκίοις φαρμάκοις)... because they do not want a child from a slave or a pauper on account of their nobility and great substance."[58]

Minucius Felix, the third-century Latin apologist, likewise contrasts the holy life of Christians with the

---

[57] John M. Riddle, *Contraception and Abortion from the Ancient World to the Renaissance* (Cambridge, MA: Harvard University Press, 1992), 106. See, also, Angus McLaren, *A History of Contraception from Antiquity to the Present Day* (Oxford: Blackwell, 1990); and Keith Hopkins, "Contraception in the Roman Empire," *Comparative Studies in Society and History* 8.1 (1965): 124–151.

[58] *Refutation of All Heresies* 9.12.25, ed. Miroslav Marcovich, *Hippolytus: Refutatio omnium haeresium*, Patristische Texte und Studien 25 (Berlin: De Gruyter, 1986), 256.

barbarities of the heathen, "who with medicines and potions squelch the source of a future human being in their own wombs and are parricides even before giving birth."[59]

The sixth-century canons of St John the Faster, Patriarch of Constantinople, likewise speak of medications (φάρμακα) related to unwanted pregnancy. Addressing specifically the difference between permanent and temporary forms of sterilization, John explains, "It is one thing to take medication so as to never bear children again. This is the most serious of all. Yet it is another thing to apply powders, which is less egregious than the former."[60] In his instructions on confession, St John thus outlines the kinds of things that a spiritual father ought to ask about. These include matters of faith, like sacrilege, heresy, and blasphemy, but also sins of the flesh and moral transgressions such as, "the desire to not have children (περὶ πόθου ἀτεκνίας)" and "taking herbs in order to not conceive (κατὰ τὰ μὴ συλλαμβάνειν)."[61] In his interpretation of Canon 21 of St John the Faster, included in the *Rudder*, St Nikodimos

---

[59] Octavius 30 (PL 3:333–334): *Sunt quae in ipsis visceribus, medicaminibus et potis, originem futuri hominis exstinguant, et parricidium faciant antequam pariant.*

[60] St John the Faster, *Libellus Poenitentialis* (PG 88:1904C).

[61] *To Those Preparing to Confess to Their Spiritual Father* (*Sermo de poenitentia*) (PG 88:1924A).

of the Holy Mountain draws attention to these texts. Whereas Canon 21, following Canon 8 of St Basil,[62] speaks specifically of medications that abort or expel the embryo, Nikodimos highlights the distinction found elsewhere in John's penitential writings: although "some women drink or consume herbs so as to never get pregnant, others kill the children, either when they have just been conceived or as soon as they give birth."[63]

Modern authors may be tempted to dismiss the relevance of the sixth-century canons of John the Faster.[64] Yet these discussions of the sacrament of confession, intended to guide penitents and confessors alike, form, according to St Nikodimos, part of the living tradition of the Church over many centuries, through their common acceptance and use.[65] Indeed, the 2000 *Basis of the Social Concept of the Russian Orthodox*

---

[62] *Pedalion*, ed. Hieromonk Agapios and Monk Nikodimos (Athens: Varvarrigou, 1886), 573 n. 1. Cf. Georgios Ralles and Michael Potlis, Σύνταγμα τῶν θείων καὶ ἱερῶν κανόνων τῶν τε ἁγίων καὶ πανευφήμων Ἀποστόλων, καὶ τῶν ἱερῶν καὶ οἰκουμενικῶν καὶ τοπικῶν Συνόδων, καὶ τῶν κατὰ μέρος ἁγίων Πατέρων, vol. 4 (Athens: Gregoris, 1854), 443. For Canon 8 of St Basil, see Ralles and Michael Potlis, Σύνταγμα τῶν θείων καὶ ἱερῶν κανόνων 4:114.

[63] *Pedalion*, 573 n. 1. Cf. *Libellus Poenitentialis* (PG 88:1904B).

[64] See, for example, *The Sacrament of Love*, 174. According to Evdokimov, the ancient canons of the Church, among which Nikodimos includes the canons of St John the Faster, are no longer relevant for adjudicating the question of contraception, though he gives no criteria or explanation for why this should be.

[65] See *Pedalion*, 562 n. 9.

Church explicitly refers to passages from these canons as authentic expressions of Orthodox ethical teaching.[66] For whereas the application of disciplinary canons may certainly vary in practice, it is universally recognized that the moral doctrine that undergirds the canons is by no means relative.[67] Yet whatever the import of these early Byzantine canons may be, it is clear that ancient and medieval ecclesiastical sources knew and condemned the practice of contraception as unchristian.

Contraception Distinguished from Abortion

In spite of the existence of patristic discussion and commentary on the moral dimensions of sexual relations and childbearing, some contemporary authors have sought to qualify the condemnation of contraception by

---

[66] "Basis of the Social Concept of the Russian Orthodox Church" 12.9.

[67] Speaking of the exercise of *oeconomia*, the future Archbishop Ieronymos I of Athens explains, "[W]here the content of the faith is concerned, whether in the domain of dogma or of ethics [the Orthodox Church] is inflexible...." (Jerome Cotsonis, "Fundamental Principles of Orthodox Morality," *The Orthodox Ethos* 1 [1964]: 240–248; 247). On the idea that the canons of the Church act as contingent historical expressions of eternal truths, see Lewis Patsavos, "The Canonical Tradition of the Orthodox Church," in Fotios Litsas, *A Companion to the Greek Orthodox Church* (New York: Greek Orthodox Archdiocese, 1984), 137–147; 143.

distinguishing pre-modern contraceptives from contemporary methods and pre-modern scientific knowledge from our superior knowledge today. Contraceptive medicines and applications, it is sometimes thought, were indistinguishable in the ancient world from abortion. "Traditionally," says Maria Gwyn McDowell, "contraception has been forbidden by Orthodox teachers; not only because of the value of children and the issue of love's openness to life, but because in antiquity contraceptives were largely synonymous with abortifacients."[68] Some writers have even insisted that what was rejected in the prohibitions against contraception was actually the murder of an already existing human being erroneously identified with the male seed.[69] The latter claim centers on a misunderstanding of ancient debates around ensoulment. Specifically, it misunderstands the ancient and medieval doctrine of traducianism, which connects the generation and transmission of the human soul with insemination and the biological matter of the parents.

If certain authors in antiquity did hold to a form of traducianism that saw all human beings as pre-existing

---

[68] Maria Gwyn McDowell, "Sexual Ethics," in *The Encyclopedia of Eastern Orthodox Christianity*, vol. 2, 571. Cf. H. Tristram Engelhardt, Jr., *The Foundations of Christian Bioethics* (Lisse: Swets and Zeitlinger, 2000), 265; Morris, *The Historic Church*, 217; Zion, *Eros and Transformation*, 241.

[69] See, for example, Morris, *The Historic Church*, 217.

in Adam in a way that connected the individual soul, as well as the body, with the biological material of the parents, it would nevertheless be a dramatic, if not comical, oversimplification to assume that the Church Fathers thought the male seed was a baby. As Noonan explains, "[U]nder no theory was the male seed itself equal to a 'man,' for under no theory was it maintained that the seed already had a soul."[70] What was far more common was the theory that saw ensoulment as being delayed to forty days of gestation, following the Aristotelian model.[71] Among those who departed from the Aristotelian model and sought to place the ensoulment of the human person at the very moment of conception was St Maximos the Confessor. Yet even for St Maximos, the human being is not to be identified with the seed of the father. Rather, the body and the soul are said by Maximos to come into being simultaneously in the womb, at the moment of fertilization, with the body deriving its origin from the underlying matter provided by both parents and the soul being infused, or *breathed*, directly by God himself.[72]

---

[70] Noonan, *Contraception*, 89.

[71] See Noonan, *Contraception*, 89–91. Cf. Marie-Hélène Congourdeau, *L'embryon et son âme dans les sources grecques (VIe siècles av. J.C.–Ve siècle apr. J.-C.)* (Paris: Association des amis du Centre d'histoire et civilisation de Byzance, 2007).

[72] See St Maximos the Confessor, *Ambigua* 7.40–42 and 42.10, ed. Nicholas Constas, *On Difficulties in the Church Fathers: The Ambigua*, 2 vols. (Cambridge, MA: Harvard University Press, 2014), 1:136–141, 2:138–141. For a discussion of this

Looking more generally at the implicit threat of killing an embryo through the taking of herbs and potions, the idea that it might not be possible to separate contraception in ancient medicine from the ethical issue of abortion is indeed problematic. Some of the texts mentioned above might even be perceived by some as condemning not contraception per se but the extinguishing of fetal life already present in the womb. This is especially true of texts which speak of contraception as *parricide*. Yet, as scholars of ancient medicine have shown, while the abortifacient nature of many contraceptives in the ancient world certainly compounded the ethical problems involved with their use, one cannot deny the distinction made in both pagan and Christian sources between actions intended to prevent conception and those intended to abort the fetus.[73] This is the distinction we saw in St Nikodimos, a distinction that was famously articulated by the Greek medical writer Soranos of Ephesos (fl. AD 98–138):

---

question as it relates to later Scholastic and Byzantine theology, see Tikhon Pino, "Hylomorphism East and West: Thomas Aquinas and Mark of Ephesos on the Body-Soul Relationship," in *Never the Twain Shall Meet? Greeks and Latins Learning from Each Other in Byzantium* (Berlin: De Gruyter, 2017), 293–309.

[73] See Riddle, *Contraception and Abortion*, 87–107; Noonan, Contraception, 17.

A contraceptive (ἀτόκιον) differs from an abortifacient (φθορίου) in that the one does not let conception take place (οὐκ ἐᾷ γενέσθαι σύλληψιν), while the other destroys what has already been conceived (φθείρει τὸ συλληφθέν). Let us therefore call the one an abortifacient (φθόριον) and the other a contraceptive (ἀτόκιον).[74]

It is for this reason that St Nikodimos can distinguish in the writings of St John the Faster two kinds of anti-pregnancy medications: contraceptives, which prevent impregnation (νὰ μὴ ἐγγαστρωθοῦν), and abortifacients, which destroy the infants that have already been conceived (φονεύουν τὰ βρέφη).[75]

St Hippolytus, too, in addition to the "anti-pregnancy medications" described above, likewise mentions a physical technique whereby women often induce miscarriage, specifically by binding themselves around the midsection. In so doing he implicitly contrasts the expulsion of the conceptus (τὰ συλλαμβανόμενα) with

---

[74] Soranos, *Gynecology* 1.60.1, ed. Johannes Ilberg, *Sorani Gynaeciorum libri IV*, Corpus medicorum Graecorum, vol. 4 (Leipzig: Teubner, 1927), 45. Cf. the translation of Owsei Temkin, *Soranus' Gynecology* (Baltimore: John Hopkins Press, 1956), 62.

[75] *Pedalion*, 573 n. 1.

the drugs used to prevent impregnation from taking place (ἀτοκίοις φαρμάκοις).[76]

The distinction between contraceptives and abortifacients holds even when the rhetoric of *murder* is used to express the gravity of contraception. As Noonan explains, "When the second- and third-century Christians apply the term 'parricide,' they do so in a conscious effort to enlarge the legal meaning to condemn what they believe is morally wrong."[77] Though this applies in the first instance to abortion, it is also applied rhetorically and morally to other forms of sexual immorality and mutilation, including homosexuality and castration. Thus St Jerome categorizes as murder even those sins that precede conception: "Some drink sterility," he says, "before [coitus] and commit the murder of a man yet unsown."[78] Once again, the issue here is not that a human being pre-exists in the form of the male seed or otherwise, but that the sin of contraception is so serious as to be tantamount to the extermination of human

---

[76] *Refutation of All Heresies* 9.12.25 (ed. Marcovich, 256).

[77] Noonan, *Contraception*, 91. Noonan points out that the killing of infants by their parents was not considered parricide in Roman law.

[78] *Epistles* 22.13 (PL 22:401). Cf. St Ambrose of Milan: "The females of our species... squelch with parricidal potions in their generative organs the pledges of their womb (*pignora sui ventris*)" (*Hexaemeron* 5.18.58; PL 14:231AB).

life. For it is precisely a human life whose generation and formation is being thwarted.[79]

St. John Chrysostom, in similar terms, condemns the avarice of the wealthy, who resort to contraception to avoid having children.

> That which is sweet and desired by all—to have children—they consider burdensome and grievous. On account of this many have even bought contraceptives (ἀτόκια) and have mutilated nature, not by aborting children in the womb, but by not even allowing their conception to begin.[80]

Here again the contraceptives in question (ἀτόκια) are medicines used to effect either sterility in the man or barrenness in the womb. As Chrysostom says in his Homilies on Romans, these are agents which carry out a "murder which *precedes coming into being* (πρὸ τῆς γενέσεως φόνος).... Indeed, it is something worse even

---

[79] The Synod of the Church of Greece speaks poignantly in this regard about children as potential saints and potential children of the heavenly Father; see "Encyclical of 1937," 332 (§20).

[80] *Homilies on Matthew* 28.5 (PG 57:357):... τό τε γλυκὺ καὶ πᾶσιν ἐπέραστον, τὸ παῖδας ἔχειν, βαρὺ καὶ ἐπαχθὲς εἶναι νομίζουσι. Πολλοὶ γοῦν καὶ ἀτοκίαν διὰ τοῦτο ὠνήσαντο, καὶ τὴν φύσιν ἐπήρωσαν, οὐκ ἀνελόντες τεχθέντας τοὺς παῖδας, ἀλλὰ μηδὲ φῦναι τὴν ἀρχὴν συγχωρήσαντες.

than murder, for it does not abort a pregnancy, but prevents even impregnation."[81]

In the canons of St John the Faster, too, a woman who sterilizes herself is said to be the murderer of children not only when she aborts them, but even when she sterilizes herself so as to never bear children again. Indeed, as we saw above, this is described as a worse sin than the taking of contraceptive powders on an ad hoc basis, because when a woman has sterilized herself "she does not know how many murders she has committed."[82]

Such is the very serious rhetoric surrounding contraception. Yet the most vivid sources demonstrating the ancient distinction between contraception and abortion are to be found in the early Christian response to Gnosticism and Manichaeism, encountered above in the writings of St Epiphanius. Gnosticism, as a heretical movement opposed especially by St Irenaeus but also by St Justin Martyr, Clement, Origen, and St Hippolytus, was infamous for its negative view of sexual reproduction, which the Gnostics considered to be the means whereby the human race perpetuated its enslavement to

---

[81] Chrysostom, *Homily on Romans* 24.4 (PG 60:626): μᾶλλον δὲ καὶ φόνου τι χεῖρον οὐδὲ γὰρ ἔχω πῶς αὐτὸ καλέσω· οὐ γὰρ τεχθέντα ἀναιρεῖ, ἀλλὰ καὶ τεχθῆναι κωλύει.

[82] *Sermo de poenitentia* (PG 88:1928CD).

the powers of evil.[83] As Epiphanius points out, this did not mean that the Gnostics necessarily refrained from sexual activity; but they did seek to separate sexual pleasure from its reproductive functions so as to avoid conception and childbearing. "Coming together," he says, "they prevent the begetting of children (τεκνοποιίαν)."[84] To the extent that this involved engaging in perverted forms of intercourse, the association of contraception with Gnosticism had little if anything to do with infanticide or abortion. Epiphanius describes the contraceptive practices and motivations of the Gnostics, who made a show of asceticism and continence, as follows:

> They pollute their body, their mind, and their soul with their lack of self-restraint. For they adopt the appearance of monks, while the women who accompany them adopt the appearance of nuns. Yet they are defiled in body because they satisfy their lust. Nevertheless, they perform the deed (to put it delicately) in the manner of Onan, the son of Judah. For just as Onan joined his body with that of Tamar

---

[83] For a thorough overview of Gnosticism, see Ilaria Ramelli, "Gnosis—Gnosticism," in Angelo di Berardino, ed., *Encyclopedia of Ancient Christianity*, vol. 2 (Downers Grove, IL: IVP Academic, 2014), 139–147. On the Gnostic opposition to procreation, and the response it elicited from the Church, see Noonan, *Contraception*, 56–106.

[84] *Panarion* 26.5.2 (GCS 25:281).

and satisfied his lust, and yet he did not complete the act by planting his seed (εἰς καταβολὴν δὲ σπέρματος) in accordance with the God-given act of childbearing (but rather did injury to himself), so, in the same way that Onan did evil do these Gnostics use their putative nuns, committing the same unlawful deed. For they place no value on chastity. Rather, what they value is a hypocritical chastity, which merely goes by the name of chastity. Their concern goes only so far as to make sure that the woman who is defiled by the alleged monk does not get pregnant. This is either to avoid bringing children into the world or to avoid being seen as unchaste by men, since they wish to be held in honor for their putative asceticism in keeping chastity. Yet whatever their intention, this is what they do. There are others, however, who seek to achieve this hypocritical honor by polluting themselves not with women, but by other means. They pollute themselves with their own hands and so imitate the aforementioned son of Judah. They contaminate the earth with their unlawful actions and polluted emissions, grinding their discharge into the earth with their feet lest their seed, as they suppose, be snatched up by unclean spirits to be used for impregnating demons.[85]

---

[85] *Panarion* 63.1.4–9, ed. K. Holl, *Epiphanius (Ancoratus und Panarion),* vol. 2, GCS 31 (Leipzig: Hinrichs, 1922), 399.

The Manichees, who eclipsed the Gnostics in the later Roman Empire, also laid a particular emphasis on the evils of sexual reproduction, which resulted in their rejection of marriage itself as evil.[86] In the face of these challenges, which denigrated marriage and at least in some cases sought to separate sexual gratification from its procreative capacity, many ecclesiastical writers advocated the indivisibility not only of marital intercourse and reproduction, but of procreation and marriage itself. As such, many Church Fathers not only defended the distinctly Christian approach to marital coupling as fecund and non-contraceptive, but they went so far as to say that procreation itself was the ultimate or only purpose of marriage.[87] We shall return to

---

[86] See J.K. Coyle, "Mani—Manicheans—Manicheism," in Berardino, *Encyclopedia of Ancient Christianity* 2:660–665. On the role of the Manichees in shaping especially Western Christian conceptions of sex and marriage, see Noonan, *Contraception*, 107–139.

[87] For some examples of loci where patristic writers speak of procreation as the purpose of marriage, see St Justin Martyr, *Apology* 1.29; Athenagoras, *Embassy* 33; Minucius Felix, *Octavius* 31.5; Clement of Alexandria, *Stromateis* 3.11.71.4, 3.7.58; id. *Pedagogue* 2.10.95.3, 2.10.93, 102; Origen, *Homilies on Genesis* 3.6; 5.4; id., *Against Celsus* 5.4; Lactantius, *Divine Institutes* 6.23.18; 6.23.2; St Ambrose, *Exposition of the Gospel According to Luke* 1.43–45; St Jerome, *On Galatians* 5; St Augustine, *Against Faustus* 15.7; St Augustine, *On Marriage and Concupiscence* 1.15.17; Caesarius of Arles, *Sermons* 1.12; St Cyril of Jerusalem, *Catecheses* 4.25; St Athanasios the

this issue below, in discussing the patristic understanding of marriage more fully. Here it suffices to note that the ethical questions surrounding contraception in the ancient Church were not merely about infanticide or abortion, but concerned sexual relations in themselves and the very nature of the sexual act.

The patristic understanding, then, like that of ancient medicine in general, was that contraception is distinct from abortion, even if the techniques and methods used then, just as those used today, were not always distinct. Church Fathers and theologians were concerned not only with the killing of the embryo but also with the purpose of insemination, the purpose of sexual pleasure, and the purpose of marital coupling. St. John Chrysostom summarizes the heart of the moral question when he asks, "Why do you sow where there shall be no reaping?"[88]

The *Oxford Dictionary of Byzantium*, summarizing what we have seen in other sources, states that, "The use of contraception was condemned by church fathers."[89] Why, then, have things changed? And why

---

Great, *Epistle to Amun* 1; St Maximos the Confessor, *Chapters on Love* 3.4, 4.66.

[88] *Homilies on Romans* 24.3 (PG 60:626).

[89] Judith Herrin and Alexander Kazhdan, "Contraception," in Alexander Kazhdan, ed., *The Oxford Dictionary of Byzantium* (New York: Oxford University Press, 1991), 527.

are we witnessing in the modern Orthodox world what Stanley Harakas has called an "exception to the [Church's] continuity of teaching"?[90]

Orthodox Christian Ethics Today

In examining the sources that have been instrumental in shaping modern thinking on this question, several principles, which purport to be "in the spirit of the Fathers," are manifest in the writings of contemporary ethicists and historians of Orthodox theology.

One increasingly commonplace sentiment is that the marriage bed, as an object of ethical scrutiny, is absolutely beyond the reach of outside interference, and, therefore, the Orthodox Church has never, and will never, issue directives on conjugal relations. "The Church Councils," says George Gabriel, "clearly respected the honour and intimacy of the marital bed, and did not legislate or permit a third party to regulate the relationship of two who became one."[91] H. Tristam

---

[90] Stanley Harakas, "The Stand of the Orthodox Church on Controversial Issues."

[91] George S. Gabriel, *You Call My Words Immodest* (Dewdney, Canada: Synaxis Press, 1995), 19, quoted in Engelhardt, *Foundations of Christian Bioethics*, 305 n. 105. Cf. Nicolas

Engelhardt avers that this is the meaning behind Canon 3 of St Dionysius of Alexandria: "Self-sufficient and married persons ought to be judges of themselves."[92] On this basis, he and others believe that prohibitions like those of the papacy against artificial birth control are foreign to the Orthodox ecclesiastical phronema. This is also the position of John Meyendorff, Nikolai Berdyaev, Demetrios Constantelos, Paul Evdokimov, and John McGuckin.[93] Expressing a sentiment similar to Griswold v. Connecticut, such scholars are of the opinion that the Church does not intrude into the privacy of the bedroom and the marital bed.[94]

Berdyaev, *The Destiny of Man*. 2nd ed. (London: Geoffrey Bles, 1954), 236.

[92] Engelhardt, *Foundations of Christian Bioethics*, 305 n. 105. Cf. Morris, *The Historic Church*, 219. For Canon 3 of St Dionysius, see Georgios Ralles and Michael Potlis, Σύνταγμα τῶν θείων καὶ ἱερῶν κανόνων τῶν τε ἁγίων καὶ πανευφήμων Ἀποστόλων, καὶ τῶν ἱερῶν καὶ οἰκουμενικῶν καὶ τοπικῶν Συνόδων, καὶ τῶν κατὰ μέρος ἁγίων Πατέρων, vol. 4 (Athens: Gregoris, 1854), 9–11; cf. *Pedalion*, 446.

[93] Cf. Meyendorff, *Marriage: An Orthodox Perspective*, 62; Evdokimov, *The Sacrament of Love*, 175; Berdyaev, *The Destiny of Man*, 235; Contantelos, *Marriage, Sexuality, and Celibacy*, 64; McGuckin, *The Orthodox Church*, 313.

[94] Griswold vs Connecticut Supreme Court 381 U.S. 479 (1965) famously articulated a Constitutional "right to privacy," barring governmental interference in marital issues related to contraception and abortion. More recently, this ruling has been extended to LGBTQ issues.

Yet, while one may sympathize with the idea that outside interference in marital relations is undesirable, and that imperious moral dictates and meddling are both unwelcome and unhelpful, the reasoning presented by such advocates is problematic. Leaving aside the warrant that one might or might not find for such sentiments in the tradition of the Church, one could ask, as a starting point, why pastoral guidance, let alone moral theology, should amount to third-party *intrusion* in a marriage? If ethical teaching offered to the married couple constitutes clerical interference and invasion, then this severely diminishes the Church's role in Christian life. Writers who insist on this point seldom indulge the reader in outlining the specific parameters of ecclesiastical involvement in the Christian home. They do not reconcile their position with the Church's frequent exhortations to marital abstinence, for example, whether during fasting periods or in preparation for holy Communion. Nor do they expound on the Church's precise function as transmitter of an ethical teaching when it is prevented from touching the subject of sexual relations altogether.

Paul Evdokimov locates the problem in the absolute artificiality and insufficiency of moral directives as a whole:

> 'Morality' has little to say here, for it is the person who is at stake, and there exist no two

identical persons in the world. The one who is immature and is satisfied with *a priori* ethics does not transcend the level of the herd, and may find adequate directives therein. But on the level of the person, nothing can be imposed on love. Love knows no moral norms. It knows normative and spiritual values where freedom and inspiration prevail; it is love that discovers these and is nourished by their revelations.[95]

This philosophy is also that of Christos Yannaras and Philip Sherrard.[96] Chrysostom Zaphiris, too, says that, "The Orthodox Church believes that the relationship of man and woman in marriage is essentially a relationship of persons. This means that sexual life must be guided by the meaning of relationship and personhood."[97] McDowell, again, states, "As unique, irreducible, and dynamic spiritual realities, personhood and relationship cannot be reduced to matters of 'natural' or 'civil' law."[98]

---

[95] Evdokimov, *The Sacrament of Love*, 179.

[96] Bishop Artemy Radoslavievich comments scathingly that, "In respect to the position of the Holy Fathers, no one can be rid of the impression that Yannaras, and other theologians with similar views, do nothing but write the theology of their own passions" ("The Mystery of Marriage in a Dogmatic Light," *Divine Ascent* 1.3/4 [November 1998]: 48–60 [59 n. 21]; Greek original in *Κληρονομία* 9.2 [July 1977]: 246–64). On Sherrard, see below.

[97] Zaphiris, "Morality of Contraception," 688.

[98] McDowell, "Sexual Ethics," 570.

Yet as poetic as these words may be, it is not clear how these views offer anything but a purely relativized approach to human behavior. Evdokimov's inclinations, in particular, appear to be derived from Berdyaev, whom Florovsky characterized as having drunk "deeply at the springs of German mysticism and philosophy," which cut him off from the life of the Church.[99] Berdyaev writes,

> The herd-mind is absolutely blind to the fact of erotic love, of love between man and woman. It simply fails to observe it and judges of the relations between the sexes merely from the physiological and social point of view. Love as such lies outside the social sphere and has no relation whatever to the community. It is absolutely individual and wholly connected with personality. It is between two persons, and any third is an intruder.[100]

We shall return to the tensions at play here further below, in discussing the question of natural law, which puts the *common*, shared nature of man, and not individual differences, at the center of moral and ascetical theology. For the moment, however, it suffices to point out that the personalist ideology outlined

[99] *Ways of Russian Theology* (Belmont, MA: Nordland Publishing Co., 1979), xiii.
[100] *The Destiny of Man*, 232–233.

by Berdyaev, Evdokimov, and others, simply fails to appreciate the Church's role in providing her children with salvific ethical teaching for upright living. Many are the times that the holy Fathers and ecumenical synods have prescribed canons for the spiritual formation and correction of their flock, simultaneously codifying the moral teaching of the Church for pastors and laity alike. These do not interfere with genuine love, but rather enable its authentic expression and exercise. To argue that the guidance of the Church, in this regard, *stands in the way* of love is to radically misunderstand the mission of the Church in the world. Only when ethical norms fail to be appropriated at the individual level, remaining on the level of legalistic and pharisaic execution, do they fail to be lifegiving.

It must be pointed out, in this regard, that the interpretation offered by Engelhardt does little justice to the context and reception of Canon 3 of St Dionysius. Canon 2 of the same saint deals with whether menstruating women should approach holy Communion. On this subject it says, "Not even they themselves, I think, being faithful and pious, would dare when in this state to approach the holy table or to touch the body and blood of Christ."[101] In this context it is evident that what

---

[101] Ralles and Michael Potlis, Σύνταγμα τῶν θείων καὶ ἱερῶν κανόνων, 7. Cf. *Pedalion*, 444.

St Dionysius understands by a person's judgment is not necessarily in keeping with what one finds today. Nor does it relate to any form of moral positivism. Rather, according to St Dionysius, it is simply the case that a faithful and pious Christian naturally acts in accordance with the piety and praxis of the Church. For this reason St Nikodimos, in his notes in the *Rudder*, understands Canon 3 ("married persons ought to be judges of themselves") to refer to a couple's abstinence from conjugal relations before holy Communion—a practice which he believes a faithful and pious couple would know to be the proper reverential behavior.[102] The spouses, therefore, "are judges of themselves" when, like the woman of Canon 2, their conscience informs them of the need to abstain from one another prior to holy Communion. Indeed, this is how the Anglican John Johnson, writing in 1731, epitomized the canon in accordance with the Greek scholiasts (Balsamon, Zonaras, et al.): "They that can contain and are aged *ought to judge for themselves. They have heard St. Paul say that they should 'for a time give themselves to prayer, and then come together again.'*"[103] This interpretation, in light of the consistency

---

[102] *Pedalion*, 445.

[103] Reproduced by Henry R. Percival, *The Seven Ecumenical Councils of the Undivided Church: Their Canons and Dogmatic Decrees*, in P. Schaff and H. Wace, eds., *Nicene and Post-Nicene Fathers of the Christian Church*, ser. 2, vol. 14 (Edinburgh: T&T Clark, 1899), 516.

that it shows with Canon 2, is much to be preferred to the modern interpretation that makes something like contraception simply a matter of individual conscience. Acting in good conscience is certainly a prerequisite for all ethical behavior, but it is not the sole criterion.

Over the course of the last century, the right to privacy has increasingly become one of the dominant factors in assessing the morality of birth control.[104] In 1984, Metropolitan Kallistos Ware had characterized the modern attitude towards contraception as leaving the matter "to the discretion of each individual couple, in consultation with the spiritual father."[105] By 1993, however, even the consultative role of the spiritual father has been abandoned, and the matter is said to be "best decided by the partners themselves, according to the guidance of their own consciences."[106] How these consciences are to be formed is not specified. Nor are we told what role the Church plays in guiding couples, who become the sole determinants of what is right and wrong.

---

[104] See Stanley Harakas, *Contemporary Moral Issues Facing the Orthodox Christian* (Minneapolis: Light and Life Publishing, 1982), 81; Constantelos, *Marriage, Sexuality, and Celibacy*, 66.

[105] Ware, *The Orthodox Church* (1984), 302.

[106] Ware, *The Orthodox Church* (1993), 296.

The Role of the Spiritual Father

In spite of these arguments that give a couple sole discretion in determining whether contraception is moral or immoral, the call for discernment under the guidance of a spiritual father nevertheless continues to be heard today.

When Pope Paul VI issued *Humanae Vitae* in 1968, condemning artificial birth control, Patriarch Athenagoras, Archbishop of Constantinople and Ecumenical Patriarch, famously celebrated the decision:

> I am completely in agreement with the Pope. Paul VI could not have expressed himself in any other way. The interests and the survival of the family and of entire nations are at stake…. The Pope's encyclical is coherent with the doctrine of the Bible. It was not possible to expect that a different position might be taken.[107]

Yet in spite of this exuberant expression of unanimity, the Ecumenical Patriarch elsewhere espouses a more familiar position, qualifying his agreement with

---

[107] Fernando Vittorino Joannes, *The Bitter Pill: Worldwide Reaction to the Encyclical* Humanae Vitae (Philadelphia: Pilgrim Press, 1970), 147.

the Pope and allowing that there might be times when contraception is perfectly permissible. "Our Church," he says, "has granted full authority to the spiritual father. It is for him, conscious of his responsibility and his mission, to give the advice and the direction that are appropriate."[108]

The idea that the moral liceity of contraception is dependent on the blessing and discretion of one's spiritual father is, of course, a very common position.[109] It is important to point out, however, that just as no ecumenical council has ever explicitly forbidden contraception, no dogmatic or canonical source has ever "granted full authority to the spiritual father," whatever that might mean. For Orthodox Christians, the spiritual father or confessor does not serve as a source of ethical relativism or positivistic moral justification. The role of the spiritual father is to help guide penitents, and all who seek paternal counsel, to fulfill the commandments of Christ in their particular situation and with an eye to their concrete conditions and circumstances. Yet in all cases it is the doctrine and canons of the Church, and not only paternal condescension, that must guide their advice.

---

[108] "Birth Control: Some Recent Orthodox Statements," *Eastern Churches Review* 2 (Spring 1968): 69–70.

[109] See Engelhardt, *Foundations of Christian Bioethics*, 300 n. 2. Cf. Zaphiris, "Morality of Contraception," 682; Constantelos, *Marriage, Sexuality, and Celibacy*, 66.

In their 1978 Encyclical, the hierarchy of the Church of Greece urged confessors not to deviate from the moral standards of Christian marriage, but to uphold the tradition of the Church and to speak with one voice on the subject of contraception:

> We call, in turn, upon the most venerable confessor priests who are tasked with the ministry of spiritual fatherhood, and we command synodically that all *say the same thing* (1 Cor 1:10) about this most serious issue, in accordance with the position outlined by the Hierarchy (in the previous Encyclical of 1937). Do not deviate from this position. You have a duty to inspire this mindset—the only truly Orthodox mindset—in all who go to confession, cultivating them in faith and hope towards God, *who will not suffer them to be tempted above what they are able, but will with the temptation also make a way to escape, that they may be able to bear it* (1 Cor 10:13).

These sentiments, as the text notes, echo the declaration of the 1937 Encyclical, which call upon the clergy to uphold their awesome responsibility for guiding married couples along the path of Christ:

> The reverend priests are not unaware that every transgression of priestly duty imposes upon the priest a grave responsibility and may

lead to such penalties as the Lord pronounced upon the wicked stewards (priests being stewards of the Mysteries) (cf. Mt 24:48–51 and Lk 12:45–46). If a spiritual father, in the matter of childbearing, reasons contrary to all that the truth of the Orthodox Church teaches and in any way consents to the rebellion perpetrated by those parents who by any means whatsoever nullify the conception and birth of children, his conduct amounts to a great criminal scandal, for which the responsibility of the priest is frightful. To him, in this situation, apply those words of the Lord, *They are blind leaders of the blind; and if the blind lead the blind, both shall fall into the ditch* (Mt 15:14).[110]

Appeals to the tradition of spiritual fatherhood, therefore, need not be calls for leniency or laxity. Bishop Athenagoras Kokkinakis, writing a decade before Patriarch Athenagoras's response to *Humanae Vitae*, also urges the involvement of the spiritual father as a distinctive element in the Church's role as ethical teacher. Yet the bishop's purpose is to stress the role of the spiritual father as teacher of the Church's traditional outlook on contraception and as moral guide in warning spouses against it. He insists that the confessor should

---

[110] "Encyclical of 1937," 332 (§ 18). See the translation below, pp. 100–101.

always be consulted in making decisions about child-bearing and family life. Like the Encyclical of 1937, Kokkinakis insists that the priest has a responsibility before God to inform the couple of the dangers of birth control, both physical and psychological.[111] Here it is significant to point out that, in his time, Kokkinakis had the reputation, as a hierarch, for being something of a modernizer, especially in his capacity within the Ecumenical Patriarchate.[112] Nevertheless, on this issue he holds faithfully to the traditional position outlined by the Church of Greece.

The role of the spiritual father is, of course, already a familiar feature of ordinary Christian life for many pious Orthodox Christians, who resort to the rich support system provided by the Church in attempting to live a godly life. For these Orthodox Christians, the counsel of a spiritual father, as a guide in particulariz-ing and applying the moral tradition of the Church to one's everyday life, need not be a call to relativize the moral law. As the hierarchy of the Church of Greece

---

[111] Bishop Athenagoras Kokkinakis of Elaia, *Parents and Priests as Servants of Redemption* (New York: Morehouse-Gorham, 1958), 57.

[112] Kontoglou called Kokkinakis a pro-ecumenist and an enemy of traditionalism; see Constantine Cavarnos, "Orthodox Ecu-menism as a Divisive Force," *Orthodox Tradition* 18.2 (2001): 22–26.

pointed out nearly a century ago, the role of the spiritual father is a critical one, and it should help couples to bear the burden of their moral responsibilities rather than serving as a perennial source of dispensation from ethical demands.

Thinking Carefully about Contraception

The ethical methodology, then, which relegates the morality of contraception to the uprightness of the conscience or the blessing of the spiritual father necessarily presumes that contraceptive methods and devices are inherently neutral, morally acceptable so long as they are used in a conscientious and well-intentioned manner, perhaps only rarely or in particular circumstances. In part, this position stems from an ethical approach which begins not with the sexual act as such, but with the moral dimensions of conjugal life as a whole. Advocates of contraception in the Orthodox Church for this reason will grant that one can by no means be entirely closed to the possibility of children. They likewise agree that the avoidance of childbearing must never be the consequence of a selfish desire for comfort, or of avarice, distrust in God's providence, or lustful indulgence. Many also insist that contraception, like abstinence, can never be imposed by one partner on the other.[113]

Yet, in the context of these provisions, it is marriage, and not the sexual act as such, which proponents say must be open to children. So long, therefore, as the motivations are neither egoistic nor faithless, contraception may be conditionally permitted. A wide range of opinions exist as to what constitutes just cause for preventing the conception of children in a marriage. Zaphiris cites "the likelihood of an unwanted pregnancy, in which case the child ceases to be a sign of [the spouses'] shared love, but risks being a burden which causes only anxiety and even hostility." He also cites "economic pressures."[114] Fr Alexander Men argues that it is simply *bestial* to have too many children,[115] while Demetrios Constantelos sets the acceptable limit at two.[116] Fr Stanley Harakas cites the need to control world population,[117] whereas Fr John

---

[113] See Meyendorff, *Marriage: An Orthodox Perspective*, 59; Constantelos, *Marriage, Sexuality, and Celibacy*, 64; Engelhardt, *Foundations of Christian Bioethics*, 235, 301 n. 104; S. Harakas, *Living the Faith: The Praxis of Eastern Orthodox Ethics* (Minneapolis: Light and Life, 1992), 135.

[114] "Morality of Contraception," 682.

[115] *Культура и духовное возрождение [Culture and Spiritual Renaissance]* (Moscow: Искусство, 1992), 445.

[116] *Marriage, Sexuality, and Celibacy,* 67.

[117] *Living the Faith,* 133. Cf. Zaphiris, "Morality of Contraception," 683; Evdokimov, *The Sacrament of Love,* 177; John

Meyendorff points to the prerequisite ability to supply "parental care, education, and *decent living*."[118] According to Bishop Athenagoras Kokkinakis, the forerunner of such views among Christians is the Episcopalian Dean Pike (1913–1969), who believed that, "There are situations in which it would be sinful to have a child."[119]

All such positions thus advocate for the possibility, if not the need, for a kind of marital 'safe sex,' in which intercourse can at least occasionally be prevented from resulting in the conception and birth of a child. On this score, the Roman Catholic Church has been accused of extreme hypocrisy for rejecting 'artificial' birth control even while accepting such practices as *natural family planning*, deemed a morally acceptable method "for the chaste limitation of offspring."[120] With natural family planning (NFP), marital intercourse is limited to the periods of time when a woman is known to be infertile

---

Breck, *The Sacred Gift of Life: Orthodox Christianity and Bioethics* (Crestwood; SVS Press: 1998), 90.

[118] *Marriage: An Orthodox Perspective*, 62; emphasis mine.

[119] Kokkinakis, *Parents and Priests*, 56–57. James Albert Pike was a somewhat controversial Episcopalian bishop who famously argued for the existence of psychic phenomena and communication with the dead. Among his writings are *If This Be Heresy* and *You and the New Morality*, both published in 1967. His advocacy on behalf of artificial birth control was featured in the January 31, 1955 issue of *Newsweek*.

[120] *Humanae Vitae*, 24.

and so avoids impregnation even while the couple enjoys otherwise normal sexual activity.

Philip Sherrard expresses the contempt of many when he says that this "may pass as an adroit piece of legalistic or moral quibbling, but it is surely a very pathetic argument with which to present the mature Christian intelligence and conscience."[121] John Meyendorff, too, asks, "Is there a real difference between the means called 'artificial' and those considered 'natural?'"[122] The present study does not seek to defend the position of the Roman Catholic Church, or even the practice of natural family planning as such. Yet it is important to point out that there is a very serious difference between periodically avoiding the fertility of the conjugal act and suppressing or destroying its fertility. As already outlined above, it is precisely this moral issue—the nullification, by interference, and destruction

---

[121] Sherrard, "Humanae Vitae: Notes on the Encyclical Letter of Pope Paul VI," *Sobornost* 5.8 (1969): 570–580 (576–77). Cf. Evdokimov, *The Sacrament of Love*, 177–178. Conversely, Bp. Athenagoras sees the Roman Catholic position as an avoidance of the problem. In this he shows his opposition to birth control as oriented toward the morality of avoiding childbirth rather than the ethics of the sexual act per se (*Parents and Priests*, 56). For other reactions to *Humanae Vitae*, see Francis Edgecumbe, "Orthodox Reactions to Humanae Vitae," *Eastern Churches Review* 2.3 (1969): 305–308.
[122] Meyendorff, *Marriage: An Orthodox Perspective*, 62.

of fertility during sexual intercourse—that concerns this paper. And it is precisely this issue that is so often completely overlooked by modern Orthodox theologians.

Chrysostom Zaphiris, although a medical doctor, does not, for one, see artificial contraception during sex as the spoliation of fertility. He speaks of it rather as prolonging "the non-fecund period which comes from God."[123] Yet the problem is precisely that, unlike the naturally non-fecund period of a woman's cycle, the extended state of infertility does not in fact come from God. If the natural occurrence of infertility is God-sent, then there is no logical reason for not seeing the recovery of fecundity, in turn, as also God-provided. Indeed, there is reason to believe that the return of fecundity is more properly the gift of God, since fertility as such is a primordial blessing and never a curse. This renewed fecundity, however, is actively obstructed by contraceptives, so that not only is a God-sent condition never actually prolonged by contraception, its artificial extension would even seem to frustrate another divine gift.

Yet whatever one concludes about the moral parity of the two states (natural fertility and infertility),

---

[123] Zaphiris, "Morality of Contraception," 683. Cf. Constantelos, who speaks of "suspending" fertility (*Marriage, Sexuality, and Celibacy*, 64).

the advantageous utilization of a natural state is unde-
niably different from the annihilation of its contrary.
More importantly, it is crucial to note that many contraceptive drugs or devices have nothing to do with a
woman's cycles but merely render sex infertile through
a variety of obstructive or destructive applications.

The distinction between the mere avoidance of
childbearing and the accomplishment thereof by the
extermination of fertility is central to providing greater
nuance and subtlety to an examination of the theological arguments for and against contraception. Indeed,
by keeping this distinction in mind, it becomes all the
more possible to appreciate the writings of the Fathers
and early ecclesiastical writers, for whom the possibility of fecundation was central to the ethics of marital
intercourse.

Sex without Consequences

In spite of the varied opinions regarding the ideal size
of a modern family or the reasons that might justify
the avoidance of pregnancy, it is generally recognized
that there exist in the lives of many couples, "especially difficult circumstances, when the avoidance of

childbearing is unavoidably imposed."[124] It is of paramount importance, therefore, to ask whether the ethical teaching of the Church, which is to say of Christ and the apostles, mediated and conveyed through the Fathers, has ever countenanced the possibility that married couples will suppress or quash the fecundity of their intercourse for the sake of 'safe sex' or 'sex without consequences.'[125]

Modern proponents of birth control in the context of the Orthodox Church have suggested that one justification for the use of contraception stems from the fact that sexual satisfaction within a marriage must not be stifled even when a couple is not in a position to welcome pregnancy.[126] This justification is predicated on the assumption that continence and self-restraint are themselves excessively onerous or even impossible. Frequent reference is made, therefore, to the apostolic dictum,

---

[124] "Encyclical of 1937," 331 (§13). See the translation below, p. 97.

[125] Chrysostom Zaphiris implies that there is such a thing as 'safe sex' or 'sex without consequences' when he says, "The use of contraceptives can facilitate a sexual life which enjoys a minimum of anxiety" ("Morality of Contraception," 682). He also speaks repeatedly of pregnancy as something "feared." Cf. Evdokimov, *The Sacrament of Love*, 176.

[126] See Zaphiris, "Morality of Contraception," 679, 682–683. Cf. Harakas, *Living the Faith*, 133; Id., *Contemporary Moral Issues*, 79.

Defraud ye not one the other, except it be with consent for a time, that ye may give yourselves to fasting and prayer; and come together again, that Satan tempt you not for your incontinency (1 Cor. 7:2). Implicit in this saying of St Paul is the evangelical wisdom that absolute continence is a gift which is not given to all (1 Cor 7:7; cf. Mt. 19:12). Indeed, St Paul is clear that prolonged abstinence is an occasion for temptation, for which married life provides legitimate relief.[127]

One cannot help but be sympathetic to these principles, which in general terms reflect the basic Christian approach to conjugal life. As St Paul explains, *It is better to marry than to burn* (1 Cor 7:9); and so the Fathers frequently speak of marriage as a remedy for fornication.[128] Nevertheless, it must be pointed out that while prolonged abstinence might indeed open one up to temptations (and the gift of perfect continence is indeed a gift from above), it is also true that self-restraint and abstinence are often an absolute necessity that is imposed by circumstance. Many are the situations, for example, in which husbands and wives are prevented from coming together, for one reason or another. There are also innumerable individuals who find themselves

---

[127] Cf. Meyendorff, *Marriage: An Orthodox Perspective*, 62.
[128] For one example, from St John Chrysostom, see below, n. 144. Cf. Noonan, *Contraception*, 77 n. 20.

unable to marry, or have not yet found a spouse. If the cross of self-control must be borne from time to time, it is not self-evident that the need to avoid conception, when such instances arise, is not yet another occasion. As the Holy Synod of the Church of Greece says,

> [Abstinence], which even medical science itself recommends, may appear rigid and unattainable. Yet it appears so only to non-Christians and those who live according to the flesh and not according to the Spirit. For true Christians, it is possible, since, in every case, *a fruit of the Spirit* received by true Christians is *self-restraint*, as the God-inspired Apostle Paul says (Gal 5:23). This is especially true for pious married couples, who receive from God the grace to confront the difficult circum-stances of conjugal life (a grace that empowers them to undertake sacrifices and self-denial). This is a most certain truth, confirmed by both ancient and contemporary experience.[129]

Indeed, it simply cannot be expected that individ-uals who find themselves racked with sexual longing or frustration will in every instance be able to satisfy their desires.

---

[129] "Encyclical of 1937," 331 (§13). See the translation below, p. 97.

In his stipulations about the temporary ascetical discipline occasionally undertaken by couples, St Paul emphasizes that abstinence cannot be one-sided—*Defraud ye not one the other, except it be with consent.* This is also the emphasis of St John Chrysostom, who notes that it is the refusal of one spouse by another which leads to immorality: "For *this kind of self-control* has produced great evils. For from thence have often arisen adulteries, fornication, and the overthrow of homes."[130] Moreover, Chrysostom is aware that man is so enslaved to the passions that he is unable of his own volition to exercise perfect continence; God must grant him this gift. Yet the fact that continence is a gift of God does not mean "there is no need of zeal on our part."[131] Indeed, St John is not opposed to the idea that a husband and wife might live a perfectly chaste life even in perpetuity.[132]

St John of Damascus, too, reminds us that satisfaction of the sexual urge is not an absolute requirement of the human person:

> Of bodily pleasures, some are natural and necessary, without which life is impossible....

---

[130] *Homilies on 1 Corinthians* 19.1 (PG 61:152); emphasis added.
[131] *Homilies on 1 Corinthians* 19.2 (PG 61:153). For similar sentiments, see Chrysostom, *On Virginity* 25; St. Gregory the Theologian, *Ethical Poems* 8; Pseudo-Clement of Rome, *Homilies* 13.18.
[132] See *Homilies on 1 Corinthians* 19.5 (PG 61:158).

Others are natural but not necessary, as, for example, natural and lawful intercourse. For though this secures the permanence of the whole race, it is still possible, without them, to live in virginity.[133]

Bishop Athenagoras Kokkinakis likewise reminds us that this chastity within marriage is a distinguishing mark of the Christian.[134] It is therefore anything but self-evident that the sex life of spouses does not admit of legitimate, if sometimes difficult, interruptions.

Fertility and the Ecstasy of Conjugal Love

More and more modern writers, however, have argued for the importance of a thriving sexual life that is not burdened by the danger of pregnancy and childbirth, not only for the alleviation of the sexual urge, but also for the necessary expression of love which sexual intercourse perfects.[135] Philip Sherrard writes in 1969,

---

[133] *Exact Exposition* 27 [2.13] (930C–931A), ed. Bonifatius Kotter, *Die Schriften des Johannes von Damaskos II: Expositio Fidei*, Patristiche Texte und Studien 12 (Berlin: De Gruyter, 1973), 80. Cf. Chrysostom, *Homilies on John* 74.3.

[134] *Parents and Priests*, 58.

[135] See Meyendorff, *Marriage: An Orthodox Perspective*, 62;

"There is a growing assertion that the physical sex act is intimately related to the mutual love between man and woman, and can serve to express this love, and increase it, quite apart from any procreative capacity it may have."[136] It is not clear where this "growing assertion" originates or whether it is thought to be in keeping with the spirit of the Church Fathers. Certainly the idea that marital intimacy is related to the love of a husband and wife, even apart from, or perhaps in addition to, its reproductive capacity, is not new. Regardless, many advocates of birth control have felt the need to explain that marriage and sex exist for more than just reproduction.[137] It is often claimed that this is the "sacramental view" of marriage, which transcends the biological determinism of the body.[138]

---

[136] Sherrard, "Humanae Vitae," 571.

[137] McGuckin, *The Orthodox Church*, 312; Harakas, *Contemporary Moral Issues*, 80–81; Constantelos, *Marriage, Sexuality, and Celibacy*, 35; Meyendorff, *Marriage: An Orthodox Perspective*, 59; Zaphiris, "Morality of Contraception," 678; cf. Berdyaev, *The Destiny of Man*, 233.

[138] Contrasted with the "sacramental view" of marriage is the supposed "natural law view," an alleged product of monasticism and Augustinianism that is said to justify married sex in its production of children and condemns contraception on the grounds that marriage and sex exist exclusively for procreation. See Harakas, *Living the Faith*, 132; Harakas, *Contemporary Moral Issues*, 79; Constantelos, *Marriage, Sexuality, and Celibacy*, 62–63; McDowell, "Sexual Ethics," 570–572; John and Lyn Breck Stages on *Life's Way: Orthodox Thinking on Bioethics*

Yet while the insistence on the sacramental nature of marriage is welcome, and while it is true that conjugal intimacy resists reduction to a merely reproductive mechanism, this point must be separated from its false corollary. For the idea that marriage is more than just baby-making does not logically entail the idea that its procreative capacity can therefore be lawfully thwarted. Implicit in this reasoning is the aforementioned assumption of the neutrality of contraceptives, whose 'noble' or qualified use provides their validation, or at the very least minimizes their general depravity.[139]

As proof that an exalted understanding of the sexual act does not of necessity involve the denigration of childbearing, we may turn to the exegesis of the third-century martyr and theologian St Methodius of Olympus. Speaking through the mouth of the virgin Theophila, a character in his dialogue, Methodius allegorically interprets the formation of Eve from the bone of Adam as an image of the ecstatic dynamism of conjugal intercourse:

(Crestwood: SVS Press, 2005), 61; Engelhardt, *Foundations of Christian Bioethics*, 300 n. 103; Zaphiris, "Morality of Contraception," 686; Meyendorff, *Marriage: An Orthodox Perspective*, 60–61; McGuckin, *The Orthodox Church*, 313, 316).

[139] It is to be lamented, in this regard, that the otherwise excellent study by Jean-Claude Larchet, *Pour une éthique de la procréation. Éléments d'anthropologie patristique* (Paris: Éditions du Cerf, 1998), misses the mark by condoning the use of contraception.

This perhaps is the mystery of the somnolent ecstasy cast upon the first-formed man, a prefiguration of man's enchantment by love, when ecstasy befalls him in his thirst for children so that, enervated (θηλυνόμενος) by the pleasures of procreation, something drawn from his flesh and bones might once again be formed into another person. For the harmony of the bodies being disturbed in the agitation of intercourse, as those who have been initiated in the rite of marriage tell us, everything marrow-like and generative in the blood (which is a kind of fluid bone) rushing together from all the members, foaming and curdling, is projected through the generative parts into the living soil of the female. And it is naturally for this reason that a man is said to leave his father and mother, altogether putting everything out of his mind at the moment when, united to his wife in affectionate embrace, he is overcome by the desire to procreate, offering his rib to the divine Creator to be taken away, that the very father might appear again in the son.[140]

Methodius's poetic and bold discourse makes it clear that an exalted vision of conjugal love need not be divorced from the question of childbearing. Indeed, one may reasonably connect the two so intimately that pregnancy becomes the supreme fruit of erotic ecstasy,

---

[140] *Symposium* 2.2 (PG 18:49).

even its driving force. St Methodius characterizes the sexual desire not as a solipsistic passion between husband and wife, but as a comprehensive longing to bear fruit and come together that they might burst forth extensions of themselves in the power of the embrace.

In similar terms, St John Chrysostom interprets the unity of man and woman in the conjugal embrace as something that is manifested in the child that their love produces:

> How do they become one flesh? As when you extract the purest element of gold and mix it with other gold, so also here the woman, receiving the richest part [of the man], poured out in pleasure, nurtures it, warms it, and, contributing her own substance, returns it as a human being. The child is a bridge. Thus the three become one flesh, the child fusing together opposites. For as two cities completely separated by a river become one by a conjoining bridge, so does it happen in marriage, but even more radically! For this bridge is made of the substance of each. And for this reason they come to constitute one thing, as a complete body is composed of a body and a head. For these are separated by a neck, or rather, not separated but joined. For since it is in the middle, it joins the two, and it becomes one and the same with them.... Indeed, for this

reason it even states precisely, not "They shall be *one flesh*," but "*into one flesh*," indicating that they are joined by the child.[141]

Elsewhere, too, when Chrysostom is at his most exalted in his discussion of *eros*, he connects it immediately with the begetting of children and the propagation of the race:

> Truly! Truly this love is more domineering than any master. Others may be vehement, but this desire is the strongest; it is undying. It is a kind of *eros* buried in our nature. And, without our noticing it, it brings like bodies together. Wherefore from the beginning woman comes from man, and henceforth from a man and a woman come other men and women.[142]

With this image one may compare the sensibilities of many modern writers, who see impregnation and human reproduction not as the pinnacle of human eros, but rather as its degradation, or at least as an attendant burden.[143] For many contemporary commentators,

---

[141] *Homilies on Colossians* 12.5 (PG 62:388). Cf. Homilies on Ephesians 20.4 (PG 62:139–140): "The father, the mother, and the child are [one] flesh, fused from the commingling of the two, for the mixing of the seeds produces a child, so that the three become one flesh.

[142] *Homilies on Ephesians* 20.1 (PG 62:135):

[143] Cf. n. 95 above.

fertility is thus seen as an obstacle to the free expression of love rather than the ground for its ultimate creativity and cooperation with the divine. Thus Nikolai Berdyaev says that, "The family belongs to the herd-man and is subject to its laws. Family life frequently cools down love."[144] Philip Sherrard, too, says that the relationship between the spiritual life of the spouses and their procreative role within the species represents a "tragic conflict."[145] Yet for theologians like St Methodius and St John Chrysostom, the begetting of children is not a lower faculty of the sexual life of spouses, but the summation and incarnation of all its goods.

Because of the obvious and natural connection between sexual activity and the conception of children, which might even be called 'sacramental' in the patristic conception, ancient ecclesiastical writers never countenance the possibility of thwarting fecundity in order to perpetuate an infertile sexual relationship between spouses. The Latin writer Lactantius strongly insists, "If anyone, on account of poverty, is not able to bring up children, he had better abstain from coming together with his wife."[146]

---

[144] *The Destiny of Man*, 236–237. He goes on to call the connection between love and procreation "fatal" (237). Cf. Evdokimov, *The Sacrament of Love*, 178–179;

[145] "Humanae Vitae," 577.

[146] *Divine Institutes* 6.20 (PL 6:709).

Caesarius of Arles likewise states, "Chastity is the sole sterility of a Christian woman." He says that otherwise the woman condemns "in herself the nature which God willed to be fecund."[147]

St Augustine, too, stipulates of the Christian marital bed, that, "Even if they are not lying together for procreation of offspring, yet the procreation of offspring is not obstructed for the sake of lust."[148]

The Authority of St John Chrysostom

Some apologists for birth control have nevertheless claimed that the authorities just mentioned are not representative of the entire Orthodox tradition. A different strain of the tradition concerning marriage, more balanced and perhaps less Augustinian, is sometimes

---

[147] *Sermons* 1.12 (ed. J Delage, *Sermons au peuple, I: Sermons 1–20.* Sources Chrétiennes 175 (Paris: Éditions du Cerf, 1971], 249): "Let her that no longer wants to have children enter into a religious agreement with her husband." Cf. 44.1; 52.4.

[148] *On Marriage and Concupiscence* 1.15.17 (PL 44:423). Bishop Athenagoras Kokkinakis likewise warns that contraception serves to objectify women as an instrument of sexual gratification (*Parents and Priests*, 58), a warning articulated in the Greek Encyclical of 1937 ("Encyclical of 1937," 330: §7).

claimed in the person of St John Chrysostom. Rending him from the broad consensus of the Fathers on this subject, modern critics point to other statements by St John wherein it is made clear that conjugal intimacy exists not merely for the procreation of children.[149] In his interpretation of 1 Corinthians 7:2, for example, Chrysostom points out that it is not the goal of Christians to secure immortality by having large numbers of children:

> If you desire children, you can get much better and more useful ones now that spiritual labor has been introduced—a better birthgiving and a better support in old age. So the reason for marrying is one: to refrain from fornication.[150]

Marriage, for Chrysostom, is not only for the procreation of children (παιδοπιία), but also for "the sharing of a common life" (ἐπὶ κοινωνίᾳ βίου).[151]

In light of the tendency to utilize St John Chrysostom to justify contraception, one cannot but sympathize with the words of St Augustine to Julian of Eclanum. Then, as now, the words of St John Chrysostom were being used to pit one element of the ecclesiastical tradition

---

[149] Meyendorff, *Marriage: An Orthodox Perspective*, 59–60; Zaphiris, "Morality of Contraception," 680.
[150] On the Verse '*On Account of Fornications*' (PG 51:213).
[151] *Homilies on 1 Thessalonians* 5.3 (PG 62:426).

against the other. In the fifth century, the subject was also one with deep implications for marriage and sexual desire, namely Pelagianism. Against the efforts of the Pelagians to marshal Chrysostom in support of their own position, Augustine responded with an invocation of the Golden-mouthed:

> Come in, St. John, come in, and sit down together with your brethren, from whom no argument and no temptation have separated you. There is need of your opinion, too, and yours most of all, for this young man thinks he has found among your writings what he believes to be proof that he has diminished and invalidated the opinions of so many of your great fellow bishops.[152]

And indeed, when we examine Chrysostom's writings in full, one finds that he is no exception to the patristic rule. Although he maintains that marital intimacy has a broader purpose than simply producing a large number of offspring, this, for him, does not justify the squelching of fecundity. We have already heard him call childbearing something "sweet" and "desired by all."[153] Indeed, we have seen him exalt childbearing as central to marital union and the ecstasy of the marital

---

[152] *Against Julian* 1.6.23 (PL 44:656).
[153] See p. 46 n. 80 above.

act. Yet some modern theologians, even when they are aware of these texts, have failed, as already noted, to connect St John's sentiments to the nature of the sexual act as such.[154]

Chrysostom, however, characterizes the destruction of seed in the womb through contraceptive medicine as an atrocity. As we have already seen, he calls this the mutilation of nature.[155] A womb which is intended by God to produce children and serve as a treasure-house of life (τὸ ταμιεῖον τῆς γενέσεως) is rendered injurious to the material designed to fertilize it. Woman, meanwhile, the gift of God to man for the begetting of children (τὴν πρὸς παιδοποιίαν δοθεῖσαν γυναῖκα), is rendered a barren instrument for sexual gratification.[156]

In the destruction of fertility Chrysostom cannot see anything but the work of the devil. He therefore comments that the drastic avoidance of children by any means necessary frequently leads to idolatry (ἐντεῦθεν καὶ εἰδωλολατρεία) and recourse to magic. Indeed, the connection between contraception and ungodly prayer is a well-known element, in pre-modern contexts, of the

---

[154] See Harakas, *Living the Faith*, 130, 132; Breck, *The Sacred Gift of Life*, 89–90; Engelhardt, *Foundations of Christian Bioethics*, 301 n. 104.

[155] *Homilies on Matthew* 28.5 (PG 57:357): τὴν φύσιν ἐπήρωσαν.

[156] *Homilies on Romans* 24.4 (PG 60:626–627). Cf. p. 46 n. 80 above.

desperate desire to indulge sexual satisfaction while at the same time avoiding procreation.[157] He that wants no offspring but cannot control himself often goes to any length to prevent children without at the same time being deprived of sexual gratification, even resorting to spells and prayer to demons (δαιμόνων κλήσεις). Chrysostom includes contraceptive drugs among these satanic measures on account of their abominable perversion of both the man and woman involved, to say nothing of the marital act itself.[158]

In light of these clarifications, one must ask with St. Augustine,

> How, then, has it been to your advantage to proffer the testimony of John of Constantinople as though he would help your case?... What has been the benefit of these words of yours except to show that either you have failed to learn the opinions and sayings of the Catholic Teachers, or, if you took the time to familiarize yourself with them, that you were attempting to deceive the ignorant by a kind of trick![159]

---

[157] Compare St. Augustine, *On Marriage and Concupiscence* 1.15.17 (PL 44:423): *sive voto malo, sive opere malo.*

[158] *Homilies on Romans* 24.4 (PG 60:626–627).

[159] *Against Julian* 1.7.29 (PL 44:660, 661). Zion is honest in facing, and therefore rejecting, St John Chrysostom's full views (see *Eros and Transformation*, 254).

Clearly for St John Chrysostom, the broader purpose of marriage, which exists as a remedy for lust, for the moral cooperation of the spouses, and for a myriad of spiritual ends, does not permit the corruption of fecundity for the sake of sexual satisfaction and intimacy. For this reason, then, the saint's writings cannot be leveraged to justify contraception.

Natural and Unnatural in the Marital Union

Obviously, it would be incorrect in light of what has been said above to infer that the legitimacy of the conjugal act was somehow dependent upon fertility.[160] As modern critics delight in pointing out, conjugal relations are often unfruitful: women are sometimes naturally barren, men are sometimes naturally sterile, the female body itself is periodically infertile, and spouses are not forbidden from coming together even in old age, when a woman is past her childbearing years.[161] The Latin apologist and rhetor Lactantius even concedes

---

[160] Cf. Zaphiris, "Morality of Contraception," 688; Zion, *Eros and Transformation*, 242.

[161] See St John Chrysostom, *Homilies on Titus* 5.2 (PG 62:689–690). St Ambrose and other Fathers have a different opinion on this issue. See, for example, his *Exposition of the Gospel According to Luke* 1.43 (PL 15:1551).

that a man might lie with his pregnant wife, though he admits this is a concession to weakness.[162] Clearly, the possibility of enjoying the marriage bed in these cases is indicative of an understanding that sexual relations are not bound by fertility; the two things are not coterminous.[163] Yet this does not in turn legitimize the conscious destruction or suppression of fecundity when it is present.

The idea that married couples should not take measures to impede fecundation is in our times dismissed as an uncertain moral principle even as the necessity of a vigorous and unhindered sex life is taken as self-evident. It is said by modern ethicists that the rejection of contraception stems not from Orthodox principles but from Roman Catholic natural law theory, which is in turn said to be a canonization of Aristotelian teleology with touches of Stoicism.[164] Yet one definition of 'natural law' in the Roman Catholic tradition

---

[162] See *Divine Institutes* 6.23 (PG 716–721).

[163] Consistent with his general esteem for marriage, Chrysostom therefore asks, "What, then? If there is no child shall the two not become one? This is simple: the intercourse effects it, their bodies mingling and pouring into one another" (*Homilies on Colossians* 12.5 [PG 62:388]).

[164] See Engelhardt, *Foundations of Christian Bioethics*, 57, 300 n. 103; Zaphiris, "Morality of Contraception," 685; Zion, *Eros and Transformation*, 253–55; McGuckin, *The Orthodox Church*, 312.

simply describes it as "the rule of conduct which is prescribed to us by the Creator in the constitution of the nature with which He has endowed us."[165]

Writers such as Sherrard and Meyendorff see in this theory a blind acceptance of "natural laws," or the laws of nature, by which they understand the determinism of matter, including gravity and other phenomena.[166] On this basis, Meyendorff asks, "Is anything 'natural' necessarily good?"[167] Clearly such an interpretation is confused. To say that man is intrinsically obedient to the divine will when he acts in accordance with the way God made him is very different from claiming that the natural movements and tendencies of created bodies are all absolute, sacrosanct, and morally resistant to interference. This is to confuse 'natural law' with the laws of nature.

Some theologians are opposed to an a priori natural law in principle. Zaphiris is the most intense advocate of what he calls moral 'synergism.'[168] "As creatures," he says, "we are obliged to obey the law set down by the

---

[165] J. Fox, "Natural Law," in *The Catholic Encyclopedia*, vol. 9 (New York: Robert Appleton Company, 1910), 76.

[166] Sherrard, "Humanae Vitae," 571–73.

[167] Meyendorff, *Marriage: An Orthodox Perspective*, 62.

[168] Zaphiris, "Morality of Contraception," 683; Zion, *Eros and Transformation*, 250.

Creator, but insofar as our obedience is an expression of our freedom, we are not passive objects of God's law, but rather creative agents of it."[169] Fr Demetrios Constantelos likewise states that, "The human person was made free, with reason and will, as well as with the ability to be a creative agent in the realm of God's world."[170]

It is hard to know what to infer from this view, unless what is meant is simply that, unlike material things and brutes we use our intelligence and free will to obey God. Regardless, it is clear that the holy Fathers have always taught that God has established divine laws, some of which he has written into the very being of man. This, of course, does not mean that Orthodox Christians are bound by Roman Catholic interpretations of natural law theory. The Latin Church possesses its own long tradition that may or may not correspond to the Orthodox understanding. Yet patristic tradition nevertheless boasts a rich history of speaking about *nature* (φύσις) in connection with moral epistemology and ethical reasoning.

In the anthropology of the Fathers, human beings sin when they act contrary to the nature with which

---

[169] "Morality of Contraception," 685. He continues: "A human being is viewed not only as a subject which receives passively the "natural law," but also as a person who plays an active role in its formation" ("Morality of Contraception," 686).

[170] *Marriage, Sexuality, and Celibacy*, 64.

God created them (παρὰ φύσιν). Conversely, they are upright and blameless before God when they walk "in accordance with" that same divinely-designed constitution (κατὰ φύσιν). "That alone is dishonorable," says St John of Damascus, "which does not have its cause in God but is our own invention, through the change from what is according to nature to what is contrary to nature, and by the downturn of our will—this is sin"[171] The "law of nature" written into man is thus breached through the *misuse* of our faculties of body and soul, or the misuse of other created things. St Maximus the Confessor explains,

> Of those things given us to use by God, some are found in the soul, some in the body, and others around the body. In the soul are its powers; in the body the sensory organs and the other members; around the body are food, money, and possessions. We are shown to be

---

[171] St. John Damascene, *On the Holy Icons* 1 (PG 94:1245). Cf. *Exact Exposition* 44 [2.30] (969B–976A): "Vice is nothing other than the privation of goodness, as darkness is the privation of light. Thus, when we abide in what is natural, we abide in virtue. But when we fall away from what is natural and come to what is unnatural, we attain the state of vice. Repentance is therefore the ascent from what is unnatural to what is natural, and from the devil to God, through asceticism and struggle" (ed. Kotter, 103–104).

either virtuous or careless in whether we use them and their accidents well or wickedly.[172]

For the same reason the first-century *Letter of Barnabas* forbids spouses to indulge their sexual desire by the *misuse* of their genital organs: "Do not be likened to them whom we hear of as committing iniquity (ἀνομίαν) with the mouth through impurity; neither come together with those who commit iniquity in impurities with the mouth."[173] St Augustine likewise states that, "When a man wishes to use a body part of the woman not allowed for this purpose, the wife is more disgraceful if she permits it with herself than if with another."[174] The generative organs therefore have their proper use. This restricts their exercise not only to lawful marriage, but even to certain bounds in relation to the body of one's spouse.

It is critical to ask whether present-day theologians who promote contraception admit the possibility

---

[172] *Chapters on Love* 2.75, ed. Ceresa-Gastaldo, *Massimo confessore. Capitoli sulla carità* (Rome: Editrice Studium, 1963), 130.
[173] *Letter of Barnabas* 10.2 (PG 2:753C–756A).
[174] *On the Good of Marriage* 11.12 (PL 40:382). Cf. St. Nikodimos: "But when it [ἀρσενοκοιτία—τὸ παρὰ φύσιν] is committed with one's own wife, it is more serious than when committed with a stranger" (*Pedalion*, 571 n. 3).

of perverting married sex in this way. Are spouses permitted in an Orthodox Christian marriage to express their mutual love physically in any form? Are the generative organs validly used for mutual stimulation outside their obviously intended boundaries? Modern authors do not indicate any reason for rejecting such a possibility. After all, they present the divinely-appointed marital act as consisting not in the deposition of seed in the womb, but in the stimulation to climax of the sexual organs. Therefore, if even when the natural outward form is preserved, a mockery is made of the process, it is natural to ask why the conventional form of physical union should matter at all.

In thinking about what is 'natural' in the marital act, it is important, therefore, to recognize that the proper use of the generative organs also demands the preservation of their God-designed function. As food exists for nutrition and health, so the generative organs, as even their name (*genitalia*) implies, exist for the purpose of procreation. This is true even if sexuality, like eating, also serves a variety of other ends. As St Maximos explains in his *Chapters on Love,*

> Scripture does not deprive us of anything given to us to use by God. Rather, it chastises the lack of moderation and corrects irrationality. For instance, it does not forbid eating,

childbearing, or having money and managing it well. Rather, it forbids gluttony, fornication, and the rest. Indeed, it does not even forbid us to think about the aforementioned things, since it is for this purpose that they were created. Rather, what is forbidden is to think about them with passion.[175]

When the things given by God, in other words, are distorted and diverted from their natural functions, in this case begetting and conceiving, this is said to be contra-natural. It is for this reason that St John Chrysostom criticizes the use of contraceptives as *mutilating* nature.[176] For the act has its limits insofar as it also has its natural function. For this reason Chrysostom also characterizes the destruction of fecundity as *battling* against God's laws.[177]

Sherrard, in his belittling of *Humanae Vitae*, points out that the Pope fails to differentiate between nature before and after the Fall—a distinction that is central to patristic anthropology and cosmology. By

---

[175] St. Maximus the Confessor, *Chapters on Love* 4.66 (ed. Ceresa-Gastaldo, 222). Cf. *Chapters on Love* 2.17, 3.3, 3.4. See, also, Breck, *The Sacred Gift of Life*, 89.

[176] See p. 46 n. 80, 77 n. 155 above.

[177] *Homilies on Romans* 24.4 (PG 60:626): τὶ ... τοῖς αὐτοῦ μάχη νόμοις;

pointing this out, Sherrard seeks to poke holes in natural law theory, predicated as it is on a fallen and corrupted condition. This is not an insignificant point. Sherrard, however, fails to draw out the implications of this distinction (between pre- and postlapsarian nature) for the Christian approach to contraception. His point is perhaps intended to highlight the existence of seemingly 'unnatural' behaviors, such as virginity or vegetarianism—things that hearken rather to Paradise than to the world as we know it and our fallen carnal bodies.[178] If so, the point certainly succeeds in highlighting that man cannot presume all his native proclivities to be perfect and holy. Indeed, the Fathers often speak of nature (φύσις) in both senses, fallen and unfallen.[179] But by hearkening to Eden, Sherrard does not find any assistance in his quest to liberate sex from reproduction. For what we find in the Garden, instead, is the exact opposite: not sexual intercourse devoid of procreation, but procreation devoid of carnal passion. This, at least, is the interpretation that many of the Fathers have given to Genesis 1:28, seeing

---

[178] Cf. St. Gregory of Nyssa, *On Virginity* 8; St. Maximos the Confessor, *Questions to Thalassius* 1.2, 21.3.

[179] For a discussion of this topic, see, especially St Maximos the Confessor, *Questions to Thalassius* 21, trans. Fr Maximos Constas, *St Maximos the Confessor, On Difficulties in Sacred Scripture: The Responses to Thalassios* (Washington, DC: Catholic University of America Press, 143–149).

the multiplication of the species as a primordial com-mandment while simultaneously seeing the physical coupling of man and wife as a postlapsarian condition (Gen 4:1).[180] If we are to really look to Paradise, then, even there we see the flowering of fertility and the bearing of children in accordance with God's law—in accordance with nature.

Conclusion

When inquirers ask what the Orthodox Church believes, it is often said that the Orthodox Church looks to the Fathers and to a continuous, even unchanged tradi-tion. According to Fr John McGuckin, the Orthodox self-understanding is that, "[T]he Great and Undivided Church is still one in doctrine and practice across the world to this very day, and that the Orthodox Church is it; unchanged in doctrine and habit from the times of the early Fathers who nurtured and kept that union with careful fidelity."[181] Why, then, should there be so much doubt about what the Orthodox Church teaches and believes when it comes to the issue of contraception?

---

[180] See St John Chrysostom, *On Virginity* 14, *Homilies on Genesis* 18.12; St John Climacus, *Ladder of Divine Ascent* 15, St. John Damascene, *Exact Exposition* 44 (2.30), St. Augustine, *On the Literal Meaning of Genesis* 1.19.30.

[181] McGuckin, *The Orthodox Church*, 253.

So long as we look to our own tradition and do not seek to conform ourselves to this world (Rom 12:2), there is little doubt about what the Orthodox Church teaches on this subject.

William Basil Zion, writing in 1992, points to the influential 1974 essay of Dr Chrysostom Zaphiris as the most cogent defense of contraception in the modern era. "His discussion is, in our opinion, the most nuanced and persuasive found in contemporary Orthodoxy."[182] Indeed, one finds little in other modern authors that goes beyond Zaphiris's revolutionary advocacy for contraception in the Orthodox Church. In reasoning about the tradition of the Fathers and the ethical teaching of the Church, the arguments made in support of birth control are generally lacking in rigor and fail to think carefully about the moral dimensions of the marital act and the nature of conjugal intercourse. Zion's own study is perhaps the most honest of recent scholarly attempts to deal with the patristic evidence. Yet neither he nor the majority of modern Orthodox authors can bring themselves to feel bound by the sensibilities of ages past. In spite of the promise to "acquire the mind of the Church" and to think with "the patristic spirit," many theologians of today simply

---

[182] Zion, *Eros and Transformation*, 248.

fail to offer an adequate, patristic response to the contemporary controversy over contraception. What we find in modern scholarship is, rather, simply in keeping with the updated mores of contemporary secular life.

For nearly two thousand years, Orthodox Christians have been clear that anything that renders bodies infertile and destroys the fecundity of the sexual act for the sake of avoiding children has no place in the Christian home. Although the Fathers often express an exalted view of marriage and the conjugal act, the ancient teachers of the faith also speak clearly and unanimously about the impropriety of sterilizing oneself and sterilizing the marriage bed in order to enjoy sexual coupling without risk of pregnancy and of childbearing. Contraception is wrong not only if and when it endangers the life of a newly-conceived child in the womb, and not only because marriage must be open to life in general, but because the marital act itself, as well as our human bodies, designed by God, admit of a proper, *natural* use.

If this traditional ecclesiastical attitude towards contraception has remained relatively muted in recent times, then it is perhaps incumbent upon the clergy and all who preach the Gospel to give renewed attention to that timeless tradition of the Church, so crucial to our Orthodox self-understanding. As we continue to seek salvation amid the challenges of the modern world, the Church alone is able to satisfy our thirst, providing not only dogmatic precision, but also substantive ethical guidance in order to help us live the life-saving commandments of Christ. And blessed is he, *whosoever shall not be offended in them* (Mt. 11:6).[183]

[183] This study is indebted to Timothy Patitsas, Associate Professor of Ethics at Holy Cross Greek Orthodox School of Theology, under whose direction the original version of this paper was written. Thanks is owed, too, to Mother Nectaria McLees, John Taylor Carr, and John-Mark Miravalle, who generously acted as conversation partners during its composition and who offered invaluable advice and feedback. I am grateful, also, to Fr Maximos Constas and Fr William Goldin for their helpful comments on earlier drafts of the essay.

1937 Encyclical of the Church of Greece

Hierarchy of the Church of Greece
To the Sacred Clergy and Pious
People of Greece[1]
14 October 1937

1 The Hierarchy of the Church of Greece has confirmed, with much sadness, that one of the more characteristic evils of our age, a tendency and development that, we must confess, is most degenerate, and which first appeared among the young people of foreign nations, namely, the avoidance of childbearing and childrearing, is attempting to insinuate itself into the Greek Christian family. It seeks to shake its foundations, to destroy the moral meaning and the lofty goal of marriage, to corrupt Greek Christian spouses, and to irreparably harm the Greek nation through the thinning of the population. The principal manifestation of this evil is what we call abortion or induced miscarriage, i.e. the murder of the embryo within the

[1] This encyclical was published in the journal of the Church of Greece, *Ekklesia* 42 (23 October 1937): 329–333. An initial draft of this translation was prepared by Hieromonk Zosimas Krampis, to which this publication is indebted. Paragraph numbers have been added for ease of reference.

womb of its mother (a murder committed in a variety of ways) and the forced removal of the premature child after its murder. Even crueler and more criminal is the rejection of infants that have just been born, and who are alive, who are then tragically label 'abandoned.'

2 Because the repetition of this evil, and greater evils still, blunts our moral sensitivity and cauterizes the conscience (so that with time the evil becomes something permanent, or at least of no concern), the Hierarchy of the Church of Greece has considered it its obligation to present the following points of urgent importance to the clergy and the people for the curtailing of this great evil.

3 It is well known that the abandonment and rejection of infants, as well as abortion, amounts to the crime of murder, not only for the Church but even according to the penal law of Greece and of all civilized nations. It is among the worst kinds of murder at that because it is committed premeditatedly, at the most far-reaching level, namely within the very family, which is the natural fountain of life. It is committed by the spouses themselves, who are thus reduced to murderers and infanticides in place of being parents, and who thereby serve corruption and death instead of shining forth life!

4 The second manifestation of this genocidal evil is the obstruction of the conception of children, known as 'neo-Malthusianism.' Through this act the spouses reject becoming parents and render their generative organs infertile and sterile, consciously nullifying and abolishing the natural law of reproduction. This crime, which sociologists outside of Christianity have characterized as "the most revolutionary practice in the history of sexual morals,"[2] and which has already spread widely around the world, threatens even our prudent and reverent nation of Greece.

5 This great and unnatural evil, therefore, namely, the avoidance of childbearing and childrearing, presents itself in these two forms, each of which encompasses a multitude of unacknowledged instances. Nevertheless, the unfailing experience of the ages teaches us that every transgression and subversion of the laws of nature has its consequences, and that all disobedience to moral laws *has received a just recompence of reward* (Hebr 2:2), according to the God-inspired assurance of the Apostle Paul. Therefore, the transgression of the laws which govern human reproduction—laws that belong not only to nature but to morality—cannot

---

[2] Walter Lippmann, *Preface to Morals* (New York: MacMillan, 1929), 291.

remain without consequences and without the punishments proper to nature and to morality.

6 The natural consequences of this transgression are confirmed by medical experts, whose opinions are summarized by two of the greatest authorities in gynecology. They write that,that "All methods of obstructing the conception of children pose a sure danger to the health of the woman," because, they say, "Nature will not be mocked."[3] Conversely, another famous gynecologist says that this act "is not only a disgrace, but the complete destruction of marriage: a danger to the health of the husband and a crime against the wife, capable of bringing about the complete extinction of the race."[4] Even more fearful are the consequences of abortions, because this crime gives rise in mothers to the most serious illnesses and even death. It suffices to note that the high mortality

---

[3] Halliday G. Sutherland, *Some Common Fallacies of Birth Prevention* (London: Simpkin and Marshall, 1928), 1–2. See, also, Hugo Sellheim's Opening Address to the 1929 Congress of German Gynecologists (May 1929).

[4] The Encyclical cites A. Damm, *De Vruchtbaarheid van Huwelijk*, 99, but the reference has not been found. Cf. Theodoor Hendrik van de Velde, *De Vruchtbaarheid van Huwelijk* (Leiden: Leidsche Uitgeversmaatschappij, 1930); and Anthony Beaujon, "De vruchtbaarheid der huwelijken in Nederland, en de oorzaken die haar bevorderen of beperken," *Bijdragen van het Statistisch Instituut* 4 (1888): 68–96.

rate of mothers who undergo abortions (tens of thousands die every year in larger European countries) has forced those who specialize in the study of these statistics to address desperate appeals to the League of Nations in order to curtail this calamity. A multitude of books has been published in Europe and America over the last few years, which, on account of these terrible consequences of the revolt against the law of reproduction, stress "the horror of racial suicide" and consider "the danger of the extinction and disappearance of the entire white race" to be imminent.

7 Yet the moral consequences are no less significant, because the laws of nature and morality are intertwined. Medical science itself characterizes the obstruction of conception as "an unnatural evil."[5] Therefore the immediate moral consequence of this evil is the disruption of spousal harmony and familial peace. This is because it is impossible for this sin, in those spouses who preserve some degree of good conscience, not to lead to inner turmoil: the reproach of the conscience. This is so because the instinct to reproduce is also a moral instinct, deeply rooted in the soul. Often there is also psychological depression, which not only destroys the peace of the family but also gives rise in the wife to serious nervous disorders, as

---

[5] Sutherland, *Some Common Fallacies*, 1–2.

the 1929 congress of psychiatrists in the Netherlands confirmed.[6] The disruption of family life is greatly increased when the one or two children to whom the spouses restricted their fertility through such criminal methods die or otherwise forsake their parents at a time in the parents' life when they are no longer able to correct their mistake by giving birth to more children. Yet an even greater moral punishment of this evil is the spousal infidelity and divorce that frequently follows. For the marriage that has been rendered sterile and infertile by such means is transformed into a disgraceful form of materialism, since it is deprived of its most basic moral element, the bearing and rearing of children, who not only adorn but also strengthen family life. Even the most fervent advocates of this perverse ideology of avoiding childbearing do not deny this truth. They confess that 'free love' will be the natural end result of their ideas, and they do not hesitate to confirm that,that "Divorce started in order to destroy marriage."[7] What is more, they themselves

---

[6] This may refer to the 1920 International Psychoanalytical Congress held in The Hague. In 1929 the International Psychoanalytical Association met in Oxford, while the 1929 International Congress of Psychology was held at Yale.

[7] Raoul de Guchteneere, *Judgment on Birth Control* (London: Sheed and Ward, 1931), 189, describing the views of Charles Vickery Drysdale. C.V. Drysdale, who opened one of the first birth control clinics in England in 1921, was the son of Charles Robert Drysdale and Alice Vickery, proponents of 'free

acknowledge that, "The public and unlimited dissemination and teaching of the use of methods to prevent conception is a depravity and guarantees calamity."[8]

8 We are not unaware that some present the financial insufficiency of parents and the medical risks of pregnancy as an excuse for the revolt against the will of God and against the eternal laws of life—a revolt accomplished through the obstruction of childbearing.

9 As regards financial insufficiency, we are obligated to point out that those who avoid the conception of children more than anyone are the wealthy classes, who certainly cannot employ this excuse. Among the other classes, we know well that there exists financial insufficiency, often even poverty, especially in this period of economic crisis. But poverty and deprivation are as old as humanity itself. Also, economic crises even greater than today's have occurred many times over the centuries. Never have economic conditions

love' and 'free unions' at the turn of the twentieth century. C.V. Drysdale is seen as the founder of neo-Malthusianism, but it is possible that Guchteneere is here referring to the father, C.R. Drysdale. In the original text, Drysdale is said to have "rejoiced at the thought" that, in his own time, "divorce had started to destroy marriage."

[8] Charles Gore, *The Prevention of Conception, Commonly Called Birth Control* (London: A.R. Mowbray, 1927), 20.

been so favorable that financial insufficiency could not be presented as a justification for opposing childbearing. Nevertheless, previous generations of Christians exhibited an admirable submission to the law of the transmission of life. Regardless, the confrontation and amelioration of the economic difficulties of a nation are never accomplished through the racial suicide brought about by the rejection of reproduction. Rather, it is accomplished through the overall improvement of life.

10 The responsibility for this improvement belongs first of all to the state. In order to reward the great benefits that families with many children provide, the state helps these families through a more just distribution of tax burdens and through the bestowal of conveniences and assistance. This is especially important because families with many children contribute the greatest portion of a country's resources, both at the material and the human level. Secondly, the responsibility for economic improvement also belongs to the individual. For there are many families that spend great sums on superfluities, on basically useless forms of luxury, and on the demands of that insatiable and world-tyrannizing deity called 'fashion.' It suffices to note that around six hundred billion drachmas are squandered in various countries every year just for cosmetics! It is a sad fact that even financially strained and poor families imitate the wealthy classes in such waste on superfluities.

11 If, on the one hand, such expenses are avoided, and, on the other hand, Christians rely on that great supplier of life, namely trust in the providence of God, which is above all economical factors and wealth, then surely the tragic revolt against the divine law of reproduction would cease. For Christians at least should never forget that it is impossible, by nature, for God, our benevolent Father, to be indifferent to the sustenance of the innocent children that we bring into the world in obedience to the law of creation. In the same way, too, we should not forget the invaluable economic significance of these divine words for a head of household who is pious and self-sufficient: *Godliness with contentment is great gain* (1 Tim 6:6).

12 As regards the medical risks of pregnancy, we remind Christians that the actual medical risks in submitting to the sacred duty of motherhood are not special dangers, such that avoiding birth-giving will assure the wife perfect health and longevity. As we noted earlier, it is incomparably more dangerous to the wife to prevent the bearing of children. At the same time, there are numerous other dangers to one's health and life that are unrelated to pregnancy, and these lurk at every step of one's life and threaten every person. Furthermore, we would like to remind Christian spouses in particular that every duty has its risks, and when a Christian avoids his duty on account of these risks, he only succumbs to dangers that are greater and more destructive.

Every Christian is called in this life to bear a cross. For those who are married, this is fatherhood and motherhood. The particular lot of the woman, which was set in place by God's first decree following the transgression of Eve, is that she bear her children in the midst of sorrow, pains, and sacrifices. Even so, Christianity provides the greatest possible consolation, a priceless reward for every Christian wife who, as a faithful and true Christian, accepts all the burdens that accompany childbearing. *The woman,* says the Apostle Paul, *shall be saved by childbearing, if they continue in faith and love and sanctification with self-control* (1 Tim 2:14–15).

13 We cannot fail to make it known to married couples that in especially difficult circumstances, when the avoidance of childbearing is unavoidably imposed, the only lawful recourse is abstinence from conjugal relations by means of self-restraint. This recourse, which even medical science itself recommends, may appear rigid and unattainable. Yet it appears so only to non-Christians and those who live according to the flesh and not according to the Spirit. For true Christians, it is possible, since, in every case, a *fruit of the Spirit* received by true Christians is *self-restraint*, as the God-inspired Apostle Paul says (Gal 5:23). This is especially true for pious married couples, who receive from God the grace to confront the difficult circumstances of conjugal life (a grace that empowers them to undertake sacrifices and self-denial). This is a most certain truth, confirmed by both ancient and contemporary experience.

14 In order to further enlighten Christians about the all-important duty of childbearing, which is being denied in the abnormal and chaotic era of today, we present a few words, first about the purpose of life and marriage, and second about the deeper causes that initiated the rebellion against this duty.

15 The fundamental problem, which has resulted in the rebellion against childbearing, is that modern man has lost all sense of the purpose of life. This is because he has set the selfish enjoyment of the pleasures of the world as the purpose of life, even though the purpose of life is the fulfillment of one's duty. And the purpose of marriage is, on the one hand, to transmit and perpetuate the human species through childbearing, while, on the other hand, providing for the mutual help and moral cooperation of the spouses, accomplished through their unity of heart and soul. Thus, in the creation of man, *The Lord God said, 'It is not good that man should be alone; let Us make him a help fit for him'* (Gen 2:18). *And God made man, male and female He made them. And God blessed them, saying, 'Increase, and multiply'* (Gen 1:27–28). It is obvious that this blessing of God upon childbearing is also His eternal and insoluble commandment. Even science, through its research, recognizes and declares that, "Pregnancy is the normal physiological function [*leitourgia*] of woman and the natural purpose of the procreative cycle."[9] For this reason marriage was exalted to the status of a Sacrament (*Mysterion*) in the New Testament. A special significance was ascribed to it through those God-inspired words of the Apostle Paul, wherein he closely compares marriage to the Great Mystery of the union of Christ with the Church (Eph 5:23, 31–32). Children, meanwhile, have also always been considered divine gifts, a blessing of God: *So shall the man be blessed that feareth the Lord,* when *his wife is as a fruitful vine on the sides of his house,* and *his sons like young olive trees planted round about his table*; and, *May he see his children's children,* says the Holy Spirit through the Psalmist (Ps 127:4, 3, 6).

16 Pious Christians should also know that the deeper cause and origin of the revolt against the natural law of reproduction is enmity against the Christian religion and Christian morals. This is why the movement against childbearing, as much in Europe as in America, has been a propaganda campaign of

---

[9] Paul Petit-Dutaillis, *Troubles fonctionnels et dystrophies al'état chronique en gynécologie* (Paris: G Doin et Cie, 1928), 337. Cf. Guchteneere, *Judgment on Birth Control*, 127.

the so-called 'atheists.' This is acknowledged even by authors outside of Christianity,[10] who confirm that the propaganda against childbirth "is a branch of a widespread movement whose work is to destroy traditional morality."[11] Collaborators in this propaganda campaign are the latest books, theater plays, and movies, which artfully teach the avoidance of familial duties and virtues. These even praise divorce and a life of pleasure-seeking. So-called 'feminist' ideologies have also played an important role. These have sought, together with the economic and socio-political liberation of women, their liberation from the duty of motherhood, since they teach women "to flee from the slavery of motherhood, from which man is also free"![12]

17 We consider the foregoing to be sufficient for demonstrating the magnitude of this crime, which is committed against the family, against Christian morals, and against the most innocent member of the human family, that is to say, the child. We therefore address, first and foremost, the most venerable priests, and especially those who are tasked with the ministry of spiritual fatherhood and administer

---

[10] For example, the agnostic American sociologist Walter Lippmann; see *Preface to Morals*, 291.

[11] Cf. Lippmann, *Preface to Morals*, 290.

[12] No citation is given in the Encyclical for the last two quotations.

the sacrament of Confession. We remind them that the tradition of the Church is consistent and has been passed on to us unchanged from the times of the apostles. It teaches that the avoidance of children is a lawless act and a deliberate resistance by man to the will of God. If, in this matter, even heterodox Churches have tried not to deviate from this tradition, all the more is faithful adherence incumbent upon us the Orthodox, the unbending custodians of the dogmatic and moral truths handed down to us from the beginning.

18 The reverend priests are not unaware that every transgression of priestly duty imposes upon the priest a grave responsibility and may lead to such penalties as the Lord pronounced upon the wicked stewards (priests being stewards of the Mysteries) (cf. Mt 24:48–51 and Lk 12:45–46). If a spiritual father, in the matter of childbearing, reasons contrary to all that the truth of the Orthodox Church teaches and in any way consents to the rebellion perpetrated by those parents who by any means whatsoever nullify the conception and birth of children, his conduct amounts to a great criminal scandal, for which the responsibility of the priest is frightful. To him, in this situation, apply those words of the Lord, *They are blind leaders of the blind; and if the blind lead the blind, both shall fall into the ditch* (Mt 15:14).

19 Secondly, we address physicians, and especially those physicians involved in the field of obstetrics and gynecology. These must be aware that they are tasked with a lofty responsibility worthy of all honor because they collaborate in the propagation of life, so that they become, in some measure, collaborators with the Creator. They are, after the parents, the most natural protectors of that innocent age, the age of childhood, and the most important laborers in the preservation of human life and the restoration of health. For this reason God accords honor to physicians: *Honor the physician, for the Lord hath made even him. And He gave men science to glorify in His wonders* (Sirach 38:1, 6). But physicians must not, as some of them unfortunately do, neglect this high calling and play the role of an assassin, performing abortions or in any way assisting in thwarting the continuation of the human species by impeding conception and childbearing. Let them reflect on the fact that Hippocrates, although living in an era of idolatry, affirmed, "I will keep pure and holy both my life and my profession." He forbade abortion to his students and placed in his Oath the promise that they would not give an 'abortive pessary' to women.[13] Today Christian physicians have given an oath

---

[13] Émile Littré, *Oeuvres complètes d'Hippocrate*, vol. 4 (Paris: Baillière, 1844), 630.

that they will practice their profession "to the glory of God and the salvation of men." How, then, in light of this, can Christian physicians degrade their field and their conscience to such a base and criminal level?

20 Finally, we address the faithful laity. We assure them that marriage is not simply a carnal union between a man and a woman. Rather, it is a calling from God for spouses to become parents. For children are not simply the natural fruit of lawful marriage, but gifts and a blessing of God to the parents. They are their glory, because, through their childbearing parents become instruments and co-workers of God in the magnum opus of His creation. This is because every child is, for his country, a potential citizen, and, for the Church, a potential saint and child of the heavenly Father.

21 We adamantly protest and absolutely condemn every method of neo-Malthusianism, which defiles the purity of family life and thwarts conception for selfish reasons, for comforts, and for luxuries. All the more we condemn abortion, because these murderous acts are a deliberate insurrection against the will of God and a revolt against His laws. No such revolt can remain unpunished by Him, as the example of Onan shows us, whom God put to death precisely for this reason. The divine Paul also assures us of this, when he says that childbearing is a means of salvation for faithful spouses such that its deliberate obstruction can only result in the loss of salvation.

22 We are not unaware of that category of parents who are faced with great difficulties in their married life, either because they bear unsustainable financial burdens or because childbearing entails a direct danger to the life of the mother. We nurture deep compassion for them. We appeal to them, however, to bear in mind that in the life of a family, as in the life of every individual, we are called to carry a cross and to suffer trials. But we must put all our hope in the power of God, who enables us to bear the weight of our cross. In these circumstances spouses have a duty to abstain, as they do in the circumstances indicated by the Apostle Paul, when he spoke of the temporary abstinence of spouses for the sake of fasting and prayer (1 Cor 6:1–6). Abstinence constitutes for spouses the only lawful means of avoiding childbearing when a real need for it is present.

23 Let Christian spouses be assured that when they are self-controlled and submissive, not to the disorderly impulses of the flesh but to the divine law, living not as carnal but as spiritual persons and accepting the burden of abstinence for the sake of the family and the exalted and moral meaning of marriage, they will thereby receive the Cross as a crown and blessing from the first Cross-bearer, our great God and Savior Jesus Christ, Whose grace and boundless mercy be with all of you. Amen.

Athens, 14 October 1937

Chrysostomos of Athens, Primate
Anthimos of Maroneia and Thassos
Eirenaios of Kassandreia
Gennadios of Thessaloniki
Spyridon of Ioannina
Germanos of Mantineia and Kynouria
Antonios of Patras
Iakovos of Mytilini
Konstantinos of Kitron
Alexandros of Zichnas
Konstantinos of Edessa
Chrysostomos of Philippi-Neapolis
Polykarpos of Beroea and Naousis
Ambrosios of Phthitis
Joakeim of Xanthos
Joakeim of Chios
Sokrates of Ierissos and the Holy Mountain
Diodoros of Sisanios and Siatisti
Prokopios of Hydra, Spetsas, and Aegina
Synesios of Thebes and Levadeia
Sypridon of Arta

Eirenaios of Samos and Icaria

Gervasios of Grevenas

Joakeim of Servias and Kozani

Hierotheos of Aetolia and Akarnania

Basileios of Drama and Philippi

Polykarpos of Trikki and Stagas

Dionysios of Sparta

Joakeim of Alexandropolis

Kallinikos of Elasson

Hierotheos of Argolides

Georgios of Paramythia

Kyrillos of Polyana and Kilkisios

Dionysios of Mithymni

Damaskinos of Corinth

Dorotheos of Larisa

Gregorios of Chalkida

Andreas of Triphylia and Olympia

Panteleimon of Karystia

Philaretos of Syros, Tinos, and Andros

Joakeim of Demetriados

Theoklitos of Kalavryta and Aigialeia

Anthimos of Thera

Vasileios of Florina

Vasileios of Sidirokastron

Demetrios of Leukas and Ithaca

Germanos of Kefallinia

Chrysostomos of Zakynthos

Prokopios of Gortynas and Megalopolis

Iakovos of Attica and Megara

Cherubim of Paronaxia

Andreas of Nikopolis and Preveza

Nikephoros of Kastoria

Germanos of Naupaktia

Athanasios of Phocis

Prokopios of Gytheion, Oitylon, and Kythira

1978 Encyclical of the Church of Greece

Synodal Encyclical of the Hierarchy
of the Church of Greece
To All the People of Greece[1]

Beloved children in the Lord,

1 Forty years ago, the Hierarchy of our Church addressed "to the holy clergy and the pious people of Greece" a message of concern and paternal admonition on an issue that is fundamental for the Greek family and for our country: the issue of declining rates of childbirth and childrearing.

2 That declaration of the Hierarchy, dating to the year 1937, confronted all of us with our responsibilities in the face of this great crisis in our country, which affects not only the family, but also our fatherland and the nation on account of the decline in population of our people.

---

[1] This encyclical was published in the journal of the Church of Greece, *Ekklesia* 22–23 (1978): 563–564.

3 This crisis is primarily a moral and social crisis. It is not unrelated to the weakening that we observe in living the Christian faith, which was lived for centuries and which made our nation great. Yet lately, the hope in *God the mighty, the living* (Ps 41:3) has disappeared from many, and this diminution *of the hope that is in us* (1 Pt 3:15) has brought about the denial of Christian moral principles and apostasy from our Christian faith.

4 A fruit of this apostasy includes the most acute problem of today: the avoidance of childbearing or the bearing of only a few children.

5 It is God's will and command, however, for us to *increase and multiply and fill the earth* (Gen 1:28). And it was to return and conform ourselves to this divine will that the voice of the Church, through its Hierarchy, called the people at that time. There is an imperative need to repeat this recommendation again today and to renew through this present proclamation what our Mother, the Church, proclaimed to her children forty years ago.

6 Over the intervening years, not only has the alarming state of affairs not stopped, on the contrary, it has gotten worse. The avoidance of

childbearing and the bearing of only a few children has achieved unbelievable proportions. And what can we say about the horrific abortions, the number of which reaches hundreds of thousands every year? This whole campaign against pregnancies has created an enormous moral quandary as well as an intense demographic and national problem.

7 Therefore, as responsible pastors of the Church, we address the following:

8 To the Government of the country and the national parliamentary representation: we call on you to avoid by all means the legalization of abortions, because these are crimes against a developing life and against the young shoots of the human race still in the womb. We call on you to not neglect the necessary initiatives and provisions for encouraging an increase in childbearing and providing relief for those who bear the burdens of pregnancy and the upbringing and rearing of children.

9 We appeal to all married men, to remind them of their obligations, that *lawful marriage and the generation of children therefrom* might faithfully follow the will of the Creator *for the help and*

succession of the human race.[2] And we exhort each and every one of you to *take up his cross* (Mt 16:24).

10 This obligation is certainly a 'cross.' But the Christian is called by Christ the Savior to take up and bear his cross, just as the Lord Himself did, and not to renounce his fundamental duties.

11 All those who *look to Jesus, the author and finisher of the faith, who for the joy that was set before Him endured the Cross* (Hebr 12:2), should not hesitate to face the burdens of family life and especially the birth of children, *who circle round about his table* (Ps 127:3). It is a great blessing and gift of God to pray *that* their *house be filled* (Lk 14:23).

12 We appeal also to women, to pious Greek Orthodox Christian women, and encourage them in a paternal spirit to sacrifice *worldly lusts* (Titus 2:12) for the sake of the family and childrearing; and to avoid all contraceptive methods and techniques whatsoever.

13 These have the duty of childbearing, *that they may do it with joy and not grieve*

---

[2] Phrases from the Wedding Service.

(Hebr 13:17), in order that they also *might have a good conscience* (Hebr 13:18)—one that is at peace and uncondemned—that God might bestow His rich blessing upon the family and *the wrath of God upon the children of disobedience* may be averted (Eph. 5, 6). d)

14 We furthermore address a warm appeal to the medical world, above all to specialists: never participate in abortions, lest you become *men of blood* (Ps 5:7). Fearing God, let the children in the womb be born (see Ex 1:17). And in accordance with your oath, avoid "abortifacient drugs."[3] Contribute, rather, through your prestige and medical influence, in encouraging pregnant women to give birth. Make only a positive contribution and provide only beneficial services to them and to society.

---

[3] Canon 8 of St Basil the Great [see St Basil, *Epistle* 188.8: "And so those women who give abortifacient drugs (ἀμβλωθρίδια διδοῦσαι φάρμακα) are themselves murderers, as well, together with those who take the embryo-killing poisons" (Roy J. Deferrari, *Saint Basil: The Letters*, vol. 1, Loeb Classical Library 243 [Cambridge, MA: Harvard University Press, 1930], 34); cf. Georgios Ralles and Michael Potlis, *Σύνταγμα τῶν θείων καὶ ἱερῶν κανόνων τῶν τε ἁγίων καὶ πανευφήμων Ἀποστόλων, καὶ τῶν ἱερῶν καὶ οἰκουμενικῶν καὶ τοπικῶν Συνόδων, καὶ τῶν κατά μέρος ἁγίων Πατέρων,* vol. 4 (Athens: Gregoris, 1854), 114.]

15 We call, in turn, upon the most venerable confessor priests who are tasked with the ministry of spiritual fatherhood, and we command synodically that *all say the same thing* (1 Cor 1:10) about this most serious issue, in accordance with the position outlined by the Hierarchy (in the previous Encyclical of 1937). Do not deviate from this position. You have a duty to inspire this mindset—the only truly Orthodox mindset—in all who go to confession, cultivating them in faith and hope towards God, *who will not suffer them to be tempted above what they are able, but will with the temptation also make a way to escape, that they may be able to bear it* (1 Cor 10:13).

16 Finally, we call upon all men and women to crusade for an increase in the number of children *according to the measure of God's gift* towards families (Eph 4:7). And we beseech you (*as though God did beseech you by us*) (2 Cor 5:20) that they hear this message with *much anguish of heart* (2 Cor 2:4). Instead of agonizing and being anxious for the future of our children and the nation, it is preferable for everyone to take up the good fight for the emergence of a greater number of children, for the benefit of our whole society.

17 The Holy Synod of the Hierarchy is not unaware that there are also difficult circumstances and problematic, and sometimes dangerous, situations in the matter of childbearing and childrearing. Either for financial reasons or because of living conditions, etc.—even for reasons of health—it is not a simple matter, and often acute problems arise.

18 In order to deal with these difficulties, many are seeking a way out. Yet the only acceptable way out for a Christian, through conjugal abstinence, is usually seen as a strait gate and a narrow way (Mt 7:14) and a heavy and unbearable burden. It is, for the majority of people, something unattainable, and *few are those who find it* (that is, *the way*). For this reason, some further dispensation and 'ecclesiastical economy' and condescension is being sought for and deemed desirable.

19 In spite of this, the delicate and sensitive conscience of Christians, both men and women, does not rest in what can be stretched and what is temporary. It remains restless despite any concessions and 'economy.' It sees it as a measure that is not valid before God and that is insecure, and *this is unprofitable* for them (Heb. 13:17), on account of the unimpeded participation and communion in divine grace and the holy Mysteries.

20 For this reason, the Holy Synod of the Hierarchy cannot take up a decision that is contrary to the sacred Canons regarding the exercise of 'ecclesiastical economy' as many are requesting for particular special cases. In such cases, if there is a real and insurmountable reason (first and foremost illness), the competent spiritual fathers will provide the appropriate dispensation by applying the provisions of the sacred Canons.

21 In all these matters, we express our warm sympathy to all the faithful and all who are earnestly fighting *the good fight of faith* (1 Tim 6:12) within the framework of the Christian family.

22 Let them be assured that for them is reserved the happiness to say with righteous exultation: *Here I am and the children which God gave me* (Hebr 2:13). For women, especially, the work of motherhood is a pillar of salvation, as the divine Apostle said: the woman *shall be saved through childbearing, if they* (the spouses) *continue in faith and love and sanctification with self-control* (1 Tim 2:15). Conversely, the children who are sacrificed and slaughtered in abortions will demand their blood from their shameless and unscrupulous parents. And this will be their condemnation.

23 Finally, blessing those families that are adorned with many beautiful children, we assure them that they will always have our practical support.

May the Lord bless our pious nation and *save* it *to the uttermost* (Hebr 7:25).

With fervent prayers,

The Hierarchy of the Church of Greece

www.ingramcontent.com/pod-product-compliance
Lightning Source LLC
Chambersburg PA
CBHW051318120626
46547CB00015B/2284